Article 38

Children in Armed Conflicts

A Commentary on the United Nations Convention on the Rights of the Child

Editors

André Alen, Johan Vande Lanotte, Eugeen Verhellen,
Fiona Ang, Eva Berghmans and Mieke Verheyde

Article 38

Children in Armed Conflicts

By

Fiona Ang

Researcher at the Catholic University
of Leuven, Belgium

MARTINUS NIJHOFF PUBLISHERS
LEIDEN • BOSTON
2005

This book is printed on acid-free paper.

A Cataloging-in-Publication record for this book is available from the Library of Congress.

Cite as: F. Ang, "Article 38. Children in Armed Conflicts", in: A. Alen, J. Vande Lanotte, E. Verhellen, F. Ang, E. Berghmans and M. Verheyde (Eds.) *A Commentary on the United Nations Convention on the Rights of the Child* (Martinus Nijhoff Publishers, Leiden, 2005).

ISSN 1574-8626
ISBN 90-04-14561-3

© 2005 by Koninklijke Brill NV, Leiden, The Netherlands.
Koninklijke Brill NV incorporates the imprints Brill Academic Publishers, Martinus Nijhoff Publishers and VSP.

Cover image by Nadia, 1 1/2 years old

http://www.brill.nl

PRINTED IN THE NETHERLANDS

CONTENTS

LIST OF ABBREVIATIONS

African Children's Charter	African Charter on the Rights and Welfare of the Child (1990)
AP1	Protocol of 8 June 1977 Additional to the Geneva Conventions of 12 August 1949, and relating to the Protection of Victims of International Armed Conflicts
AP2	Protocol of 8 June 1977 Additional to the Geneva Conventions of 12 August 1949, and relating to the Protection of Victims of Non-International Armed Conflicts
AU	African Union
CCPR	International Covenant on Civil and Political Rights
CRC	Convention on the Rights of the Child
CRC Committee	Committee on the Rights of the Child
Child Soldiers Protocol	Optional Protocol to the Convention on the Rights of the Child on the involvement of children in armed conflict of 25 May 2000
EU	European Union
GC1	Geneva Convention (I) of 12 August 1949 for the Amelioration of the Condition of the Wounded and Sick in Armed Forces in the Field
GC2	Geneva Convention (II) of 12 August 1949 for the Amelioration of the Condition of Wounded, Sick and Shipwrecked Members of Armed Forces at Sea
GC3	Geneva Convention (III) of 12 August 1949 relative to the Treatment of Prisoners of War
GC4	Geneva Convention (IV) of 12 August 1949 relative to the Protection of Civilian Persons in Time of War (GC4).
ICC	International Criminal Court
ICJ	International Court of Justice
ICRC	International Committee of the Red Cross

IHL	International humanitarian law
ILO	International Labour Organization
NGO	Non-governmental Organization
OAS	Organization of American States
SC	Security Council
UN	United Nations
UNICEF	United Nations Children's Fund
USA	United States of America

AUTHOR BIOGRAPHY

Fiona Ang is a Belgian researcher. She currently works as a PhD researcher at the Catholic University of Leuven. She is involved in an interuniversity and interdisciplinary project on the UN Convention on the Rights of the Child and conducts research on the human rights framework applicable to children with a psychiatric disorder. Previously, she studied law at the Catholic University of Leuven (K.U. Leuven, Belgium) and Northwestern University (Chicago, USA). As a law student, she was a member of the winning team of the 'Jean-Pictet' competition—an international moot court on international humanitarian law (Cleveland, USA and Geneva, Switzerland). After obtaining her law degree, she fulfilled internships with Amnesty International at its UN office in Geneva (Switzerland) and with the International Labour Organisation in Jakarta (Indonesia), where she participated in the International Programme on the Eradication of Child Labour.

TEXT OF ARTICLE 38

ARTICLE 38

1. States Parties undertake to respect and to ensure respect for rules of international humanitarian law applicable to them in armed conflicts which are relevant to the child.

2. States Parties shall take all feasible measures to ensure that persons who have not attained the age of fifteen years do not take a direct part in hostilities.

3. States Parties shall refrain from recruiting any person who has not attained the age of fifteen years into their armed forces. In recruiting among those persons who have attained the age of fifteen years but who have not attained the age of eighteen years, States Parties shall endeavour to give priority to those who are oldest.

4. In accordance with their obligations under international humanitarian law to protect the civilian population in armed conflicts, States Parties shall take all feasible measures to ensure protection and care of children who are affected by an armed conflict.

ARTICLE 38

1. Les Etats parties s'engagent à respecter et à faire respecter les règles du droit humanitaire international qui leur sont applicables en cas de conflit armé et dont la protection s'étend aux enfants.

2. Les Etats parties prennent toutes les mesures possibles dans la pratique pour veiller à ce que les personnes n'ayant pas atteint l'âge de quinze ans ne participent pas directement aux hostilités.

3. Les Etats parties s'abstiennent d'enrôler dans leurs forces armées toute personne n'ayant pas atteint l'âge de quinze ans. Lorsqu'ils incorporent des personnes de plus de quinze ans mais de moins de dix-huit ans, les Etats parties s'efforcent d'enrôler en priorité les plus âgées.

4. Conformément à l'obligation qui leur incombe en vertu du droit humanitaire international de protéger la population civile en cas de conflit armé, les Etats parties prennent toutes les mesures possibles dans la pratique pour que les enfants qui sont touchés par un conflit armé bénéficient d'une protection et de soins.

CHAPTER ONE

INTRODUCTION*

1. Article 38 of the UN Convention on the Rights of the Child (CRC)[1] deals
with the situation of children in armed conflicts. This is clearly a politically
trendy issue: new legal instruments—such as the Child Soldiers Protocol[2]—
are created, and the Security Council has started to practically annually
adopt related resolutions.[3] This worldwide attention is not surprising. During
the 1990s, more than 8 million children have died, been permanently disabled or seriously injured as a result of armed conflicts.[4] As described in
her groundbreaking report, UN appointed expert Graça Machel has extensively outlined the disastrous effects armed conflicts have on children.[5]
Hence, it is obvious that children caught up in an armed conflict constitute
a group particularly vulnerable to human rights violations, which explains
the inclusion of Article 38 in the CRC. This contribution will first briefly
compare Article 38 to related universal and regional human rights provisions, after which a detailed analysis will be made of the meaning of the
terms used in this article.

---

* 1 September 2004, with the exception of the reference to the ICRC study on customary
international humanitarian law (*cf. infra* No. 21). I would like to warmly thank Heidi Pauken
and Michael Duttwiler (Pictct coaches for life) for their support and very useful comments.
  [1] Adopted by UN General Assembly Resolution 44/25 of 20 November 1989, entered into
force 2 September 1990.
  [2] Optional Protocol to the Convention on the Rights of the Child on the involvement of
children in armed conflict of 25 May 2000, entered into force 12 February 2002.
  [3] Security Council Resolutions 1539 (2004), 1460 (2003), 1379 (2001), 1314 (2000), 1261 (1999).
  [4] G. Machel, *The Impact of Armed Conflict on Children: A critical review of progress made and
obstacles encountered in increasing protection of war-affected children*, available at <http://www.war-
affectedchildren.gc.ca>.
  [5] G. Machel, *The Impact of Armed Conflict on Children* (UN Doc. A/51/306, 1996).

CHAPTER TWO

COMPARISON WITH RELATED INTERNATIONAL
HUMAN RIGHTS PROVISIONS

1. *Universal Human Rights Law*

2. Within the universal human rights system, the CRC is rather exceptional since it includes a provision that traditionally belongs to the field of international humanitarian law (IHL).[6] In this perspective, it is clear that the drafters of the CRC have opted for the creation of an instrument that is holistic at different levels. It is commonly known that the CRC covers both civil and political rights and economic, social and cultural rights, which—despite the apparent divergence regarding enforceability[7]—rightly applies the official United Nations doctrine on the indivisibility, interdependence and interrelatedness of all human rights.[8] But the CRC also brings together two branches of public international law that are usually dealt with separately: human rights law and IHL.[9] The only similar universal human rights instrument, uniting human rights and IHL, is the Child Soldiers Protocol. This Protocol elaborates the second and third paragraph of Article 38 of the CRC, as will be outlined in Sections 3 to 5 of Chapter III.

2. *Regional Human Rights Law*

3. The fully integrated approach adopted by the CRC towards the rights of the child as described above, has proven a fruitful source of inspiration[10]

---

[6] S. Detrick, *A Commentary on the Convention on the Rights of the Child* (The Hague, Kluwer Law International, 1999) p. 647.

[7] Article of the 4 CRC; D. Mzikenge Chirwa, 'The merits and demerits of the African Children's Charter on the Rights and Welfare of the Child', *The International Journal of Children's Rights* 10, No. 2, 2002, p. 158.

[8] Vienna Declaration and Programme of Action adopted by the World Conference on Human Rights in Vienna, 25 June 1993, para. 5.

[9] On the relation human rights—IHL: *cf. infra* Introduction to Chapter III.

[10] D. Mzikenge Chirwa, 'The merits and demerits of the African Children's Charter on the Rights and Welfare of the Child', *l.c.* (note 7), p. 157; D. Olowu, 'Protecting Children's Rights in Africa: A critique of the African Children's Charter on the Rights and Welfare of the Child', *The International Journal of Children's Rights* 10, No. 2, 2002, p. 128.

for the drafters of the African Children's Charter on the Rights and Welfare of the Child.[11] Of the different regional human rights systems, the African Union is the only one with a legally binding instrument on children's rights that also deals with IHL, as will be illustrated below.

4. *Europe.* At the European level, the Council of Europe only has a European Convention on the Exercise of Children's Rights,[12] which is merely dedicated to procedural issues related to the participation of children in court procedures where the interests of the child are at stake.[13] As for the European Union (EU), the European Parliament has adopted a Resolution on a Charter of Rights of the Child,[14] addressing some problems specifically related to children in the EU.[15] In general, the proposed Charter largely confirms the provisions laid down in the CRC, with, however, an unfortunate exception for Article 38 of the CRC, the provisions of which have been entirely omitted. Though likewise not binding, yet noteworthy are the European Parliament Resolution on Child Soldiers[16] and, especially, the EU Guidelines on Children and Armed Conflict, issued by the Council of the EU.[17] In the latter, the Council of the EU declares that '[t]he EU's objective is to influence third countries and non-State actors to implement international human rights norms and standards and humanitarian law, as well as regional international human rights law instruments [. . .] and to take effective measures to protect children from the effects of armed conflict, to end the use of children in armies and armed groups, and to end impunity'.[18] This wording is reminiscent of Article 38 of the CRC.

5. *The Americas.* Although there is no specific instrument on children's rights within the Organisation of American States (OAS), the Inter-American Commission on Human Rights has taken up the issue of child soldiers.[19] Also

---

[11] AU Doc. CAB/LEG/24.9/49 (1990), entered into force 29 November 1999 (hereinafter: the African Children's Charter).

[12] European Convention on the Exercise of Children's Rights, ETS No. 160, entered into force 1 July 2000.

[13] Explanatory Report to the European Convention on the Exercise of Children's Rights, para. 3.

[14] European Parliament, Resolution on a European Charter of Rights of the Child of 8 July 1992, *Official Journal*, C 241, 21 September 1992, p. 67.

[15] *E.g.* 'freedom of movement throughout the territory of the Community', as provided in Article 8.18 of the proposed Charter.

[16] Resolution B4-1078, 17 December 1998.

[17] Council of the European Union, 4 December 2003.

[18] Para. 6.

[19] *E.g.* in its 1999 Annual Report (Annual Report of the Inter-American Commission on

to the General Assembly of the OAS, IHL is important: every year, it adopts a resolution covering the promotion of and respect for this branch of law,[20] sometimes even specifically dealing with children and armed conflicts.[21] Interesting to note in this respect, are the decisions of the Inter-American Commission on Human Rights directly examining State compliance with IHL.[22] In spite of the Inter-American Court on Human Rights' ruling[23] that both Commission and Court are competent to monitor compliance with the American Convention on Human Rights only,[24] and not with IHL, scholars believe that the 'importance of humanitarian law for the effective protection of human rights in the Americas remains very much intact'.[25]

6. *Africa.* As mentioned above, the only legally binding regional human rights instrument containing an IHL provision is the African Children's Charter. Its Article 22 is to a large extent similar to Article 38 of the CRC, since both encompass the rules of IHL,[26] prohibit the direct participation of children in hostilities,[27] and oblige the States Parties to protect the civilian population.[28] In the analysis of the exact meaning of Article 38 of the CRC in Chapter III, a detailed comparison will be made with the African Children's Charter, but it is already worth mentioning a few significant differences here.

Contrary to the formulation used in Article 38 *juncto* Article 1 of the CRC, the African Children's Charter puts forward a watertight prohibition on the recruitment and participation of persons below 18 years of age,[29] which is

---

Human Rights 1999, Chapter 6, Recommendation for eradicating the recruitment of children and their participation in armed conflicts, OEA/Ser.L/V/II.106 Doc. 6 April 13, 1999).

[20] *E.g.* AG/RES. 1944 (XXXIII-O/03, adopted on 10 June 2003) and AG/RES. 1904 (XXXII-O/02, adopted on 4 June 2002).

[21] AG/RES. 1709 (XXX-O/00), adopted on 5 June 2000.

[22] Inter-American Commission on Human Rights, *Avilán et al. v. Colombia*, Report N. 26/97, Case 11.142, Inter-Am. C.H.R. 444, OEA/Ser.L/V/II.98, doc. 6 rev. (1998); Inter-American Commission on Human Rights, *Hugo Bustíos Saavedra v. Peru*, Report No. 38/97, Case 103548, Inter-Am. C.H.R. 753, OEA/ser.L/V/II.98, doc. 6 rev. (1998); Inter-American Commission on Human Rights, *Juan Carlos Abella v. Argentina*, Report No. 55/97, Case 11.137, Inter-Am. C.H.R. 271, OEA ser.L/V/II.98, doc. 6 rev. (1998).

[23] Inter-American Court on Human Rights, *Las Palmeras*, Preliminary Objections, Judgement, 4 February 2000, Series C: Decisions and Judgements No. 67, para. 33.

[24] Adopted on 22 November 1969 (O.A.S.T.S. No. 36, O.A.S. Off. Rec. OEA/Ser.L/V/II.78, doc. 21, rev. 6 (1979), entered into force 18 July 1978).

[25] L. Moir, 'International Humanitarian Law and the Inter-American Human Rights System', *Human Rights Quarterly* 25, 2003, p. 212.

[26] Article 38 para. 1 of the CRC and Article 22 para. 1 of the African Children's Charter.

[27] Article 38 paras. 2–3 of the CRC and Article 22 para. 2 of the African Children's Charter.

[28] Article 38 para. 4 of the CRC and Article 22 para. 3 of the African Children's Charter.

[29] K.C.J.M. Arts, 'The International Protection of Children's Rights in Africa: the 1990 AU Charter on the Rights and Welfare of the Child', *The African Journal of International and Comparative Law* I, No. 5, 1993, p. 152.

the highest standard of all international legal systems.[30] Moreover, bearing in mind the relatively high frequency of internal tensions on the African continent, it is particularly interesting that the protection of civilians not only ought to be guaranteed in 'armed conflicts'—which means that a rather high threshold of violence should be reached in order to trigger the applicability of IHL, as is the case with Article 38 of the CRC—but also in 'tensions and strives'.[31] This is a clear example of the potential of regional children's rights instruments: complementary to the universal CRC,[32] the African Children's Charter shows the priorities of a region ravaged by conflicts and other disasters which make daily life so difficult for all too many African children.[33]

7. Although the practical impact of the African Children's Charter in general remains of course yet to be seen, it is encouraging to notice that some States that are not a party to other relevant instruments, did ratify the African Children's Charter.[34] The possibility of violations of the African Children's Charter being brought before the African Commission on Human and Peoples' Rights, which has been suggested by scholars,[35] could open new perspectives as to the monitoring and enforcement mechanisms of the African Children's Charter. And despite the often heard criticism of ineffectiveness and immaturity, the African Children's Charter in particular and the AU human rights system in general should be 'lauded for being the most forward thinking of all the regional systems, and for having the capacity to add to the development of international human rights law',[36] as will be illustrated in the next Chapter.

---

[30] D. Mzikenge Chirwa, 'The merits and demerits of the African Children's Charter on the Rights and Welfare of the Child', *l.c.* (note 7), p. 168.

[31] *Cf. infra* No. 28–29.

[32] K.C.J.M. Arts, 'The International Protection of Children's Rights in Africa: the 1990 AU Charter on the Rights and Welfare of the Child', *l.c.* (note 29), p. 144; D. Olowu, 'Protecting Children's Rights in Africa: A critique of the African Children's Charter on the Rights and Welfare of the Child', *l.c.* (note 10), p. 128.

[33] H. Gherari, 'La Charte africaine des droits et du bien-être de l'enfant', *Etudes internationales* (Institut canadien des affaires internationales) XXII, No. 4, 1991, p. 736.

[34] *E.g.* Angola is only a party to the 1949 Geneva Conventions, their First Additional Protocol (AP1) and ILO Convention 182 concerning the Prohibition and Immediate Action for the Elimination of the Worst Forms of Child Labour of 17 June 1999, entered into force 19 November 2000 (ILO Convention 182) yet not to the Second Additional Protocol to the Geneva Conventions; Eritrea is only a party to the 1949 Geneva Conventions.

[35] D. Olowu, 'Protecting Children's Rights in Africa: A critique of the African Children's Charter on the Rights and Welfare of the Child', *l.c.* (note 10), p. 133.

[36] A. Lloyd, 'Evolution of the African Children's Charter on the Rights and Welfare of the Child and the African Committee of Experts: Raising the gauntlet', *The International Journal of Children's Rights* 10, No. 2, 2002, p. 179.

8. It can be concluded that at the international and to a large extent also regional level, there are no 'related *international human rights* provisions' regarding Article 38 of the CRC. The legal texts to which this article could— and with a view to the CRC's saving clause which mentions 'international law' in general,[37] should—be compared, are to be looked for in the field of IHL. As Article 38 §1 of the CRC explicitly refers to the obligation for States Parties to 'respect and ensure respect for rules of IHL', an analysis of State obligations under Article 38 automatically leads to a study of these 'rules of IHL': the latter form an integral part of the law that should be complied with under Article 38 of the CRC. Therefore, Chapter III will consist of a discussion on Article 38 of the CRC including the rules of IHL that are relevant to the child.

---

[37] Article 41 of the CRC: 'Nothing in the present Convention shall affect any provisions which are more conducive to the realization of the rights of the child and which may be contained in: (a) The law of a State party; or (b) International law in force for that State'.

CHAPTER THREE

SCOPE OF ARTICLE 38

1. *Introduction*

9. As mentioned above, Article 38 of the CRC has a hybrid character. Materially speaking, Article 38 of the CRC is clearly an IHL provision.[38] Yet formally speaking, Article 38 is part of a human rights instrument. Without doubting the undeniable value of the mere existence of this article, emphasis should be put on the fact that it is far from self-evident to mix both bodies of law. At least historically, these branches of public international law have developed separately and distinctly from each other,[39] which resulted in separate and distinct systems in the field of, among others, interpretation, monitoring and enforcement. The way in which these systems are different therefore should be examined: only then, an assessment can be made of the implications resulting from those differences with regard to the interpretation and application of Article 38 of the CRC.

1.1. *IHL and Human Rights*

10. According to the concept of human rights, every human being is entitled to something, by simple virtue of being a human being.[40] Human rights are universal (belonging 'to each of us regardless of ethnicity, race, gender, sexuality, age, religion, political conviction, or type of government')[41] and subjective (being 'the properties of individual subjects').[42] They are laid down in a set of United Nations treaties and various constitutions around the world.

11. IHL, on the other hand, is according to the International Committee on the Red Cross (ICRC)—the most authoritative source for the interpretation

---

[38] *Cf. infra* No. 16.
[39] L. Doswald-Beck and S. Vité, 'International Humanitarian Law and Human Rights Law', *International Review of the Red Cross*, No. 293, 1993, p. 94.
[40] M. Piechowiak, 'What are Human Rights? The Concept of Human Rights and Their Extra-Legal Justification', in R. Hanski and M. Suksi (eds.), *An Introduction to the International Protection of Human Rights* (Turku/Åbo, Institute for Human Rights, 1999), p. 3.
[41] D.J. O'Byrne, *Human Rights: an introduction* (Harlow, Prentice Hall, 2003), p. 27.
[42] *Ibid.*

of IHL—'a set of international rules, established by treaty or custom, which are specifically intended to solve humanitarian problems directly arising from international or non-international armed conflicts. It protects persons and property that are, or may be, affected by an armed conflict and limits the right of the parties to a conflict to use methods and means of warfare of their choice'.[43]

12. This implies the first and most visible divergence between IHL and international human rights law: whereas the latter in principle applies in all circumstances, IHL is only applicable in times of armed conflict.[44] As will be discussed in Subsection 2.1.2, the threshold of violence needed to trigger the applicability of IHL is always somewhat arbitrary since, in most cases, the characterisation of the situation depends on the State(s) involved. This often leads to an official denial of the existence of an armed conflict, and thus of the applicability of IHL.

Fortunately, international human rights law is applicable at all times, be it a time of peace, of armed conflict, or of any other kind of violent disturbances. There is an exception, however, as a derogation clause may suspend the applicability of certain human rights in case of a public emergency threatening the life of the nation.[45] But—apart from the relatively strict derogation conditions—[46] even then, a core of 'non-derogable' human rights is still to be respected. This core includes the prohibition of slavery, torture, racial discrimination and genocide.[47] If no such derogation has been made, international human rights law remains to be applicable, as was confirmed in the 1970 UN General Assembly resolution 2675 (XXV).[48]

13. Secondly, this difference in scope of application between IHL and international human rights law is reinforced by the difference in monitoring and enforcement mechanisms—although a shared element could be the

---

[43] International Committee of the Red Cross, *What is International Humanitarian Law? A Fact Sheet*, available at <http://www.icrc.org/Web/Eng/siteeng0.nsf/htmlall/57JNXM/$FILE/What_is_IHL.pdf?OpenElement>.

[44] A. Eide, 'The laws of war and human rights: Differences and convergences', in: C. Swinarski (ed.), *Etudes et essais sur le droit international humanitaire et sur les principes de la Croix-Rouge en l'honneur de Jean Pictet* (Geneva, Comité international de la Croix-Rouge, 1984), p. 680.

[45] Cf. e.g. Article 4 of the CCPR.

[46] Human Rights Committee, *General Comment No. 29: States of Emergency 2001* (UN Doc. CCPR/C/21/Rev.1/Add.11, 2001).

[47] M.N. Shaw, *International Law* (Cambridge, Cambridge University Press, 2003), p. 116.

[48] Article 1: '[F]undamental human rights, as accepted in international law and laid down in international instruments, continue to apply fully in situations of armed conflict'.

deplorable yet common perception that both bodies of law are only weakly enforceable.

State compliance with IHL is mostly monitored by the ICRC. In times of armed conflict, an 'external' State can be appointed 'Protecting Power', supervising this compliance,[49] yet *de facto* this role is normally fulfilled by the ICRC.[50] The latter also assists States in implementing the various IHL instruments.[51] Vital part of this implementation legislation is the criminalisation of certain violations of IHL. The so-called 'grave breaches' are exhaustively enumerated in the Geneva Conventions and AP1 and lead to individual criminal responsibility.[52] These war crimes have been included in international treaties such as the statutes of the *ad hoc* international criminal tribunals and the International Criminal Court.

It is remarkable that this international criminal law approach is increasingly also adopted towards serious human rights violations. The importance of domestic legislation implementing the State human rights obligations is comparable to that in the case of IHL.[53] Yet very different is the main monitoring mechanism in place:[54] States that are a party to the UN human rights treaties commit themselves to report on a regular basis to a specifically appointed UN treaty body on how and to what extent they have realized the provisions of those treaties.[55] Although the 'concluding observations' of those treaty bodies are not legally binding, they carry a strong moral and political authority, stimulating States to do better wherever needed. In this perspective, one could say that human rights law is enforced in a more pressing way than IHL, which, as previously described, does not entail any reporting obligation for States.

---

[49] Article 8 of the GC1, GC2 and GC3; Article 9 of the GC4.

[50] F. Kalshoven and L. Zegveld, *Constraints on the Waging of War* (Geneva, International Committee of the Red Cross, 2001), p. 73.

[51] As obliged under Article 80 para. 1 of the Protocol of 8 June 1977 Additional to the Geneva Conventions of 12 August 1949, and relating to the Protection of Victims of International Armed Conflicts (AP1).

[52] *Cf. infra* No. 55.

[53] Although certain provisions of human rights treaties, including the CRC, might be self-executing: A. Vandaele and W. Pas, 'International Human Rights Treaties and their Relation with National Law: Monism, Dualism and the Self-executing Character of Human Rights, in: E. Verhellen and A. Weyts (eds.), *Understanding Children's Rights 2003* (Gent, Children's Rights Centre, Ghent University, 2004), pp. 384–393.

[54] Not covered: individual complaints mechanism and Commission on Human Rights procedures.

[55] M.N. Shaw, *o.c.* (note 47), pp. 290–310.

14. Finally, what appears to render a reconciliation of IHL and human rights fundamentally impossible, is the fact that IHL allows the killing and wounding of combatants and, under certain conditions, even civilians: as long as the 'rules of the game' are observed between the formally equal parties to the conflict, it is permissible to cause suffering or even to kill.[56] At the other side of the spectrum, so it seems, there is human rights law protecting the weak governed from their strong governments, whereby no one may be deprived of life (except if the death penalty is still in use).[57] In fact, a consistent approach from the human rights angle would be to prevent and stop all armed conflicts since they are intrinsically irreconcilable with the respect for human rights. The CRC Committee does not even hesitate to actually call upon States to end the armed conflict they are involved in.[58] As the question of legitimacy of the beginning of an armed conflict belongs to *ius ad bellum*, which is to be distinguished from *ius in bello* or IHL, it is clear that the latter, on the other hand, takes the existence of armed conflict for granted.

15. Still, tendencies towards a far-reaching convergence between IHL and international human rights law seem to be emerging. The ICRC maintains that both branches of public international law are 'distinct yet related',[59] while some scholars advocate the inclusion of human rights law in IHL.[60] Others argue it should be the other way around. But the common denominator of each of those 3 theories is that both are not mutually exclusive: human rights—also economic, social and cultural rights[61]—continue to apply in armed conflict, even if a derogation declaration has been made. In fact, the CRC does not even have a derogation clause. Although there is some disagreement regarding the meaning of this omission,[62] the main tendency

---

[56] T. Meron, 'The Humanization of Humanitarian Law', *American Journal of International Law* 94, No. 2, 2000, p. 240.

[57] *E.g.* Article 6 of the CCPR.

[58] *E.g.* CRC Committee, *Concluding Observations: Myanmar* (UN Doc. CRC/C/15/Add.237, 2004), para. 67.

[59] International Committee of the Red Cross, *International Humanitarian Law and International Human Rights Law: Similarities and Differences*, available at <http://www.icrc.org/Web/Eng/siteeng0.nsf/htmlall/57JR8L/$FILE/IHL_and_IHRL.pdf?OpenElement>.

[60] E. Chadwick, '"Rights" and International Humanitarian Law', in: C. Gearty and A. Tomkins (eds.), *Understanding Human Rights* (London/New York, Mansell, 1996), p. 573.

[61] R. Provost, *International Human Rights and Humanitarian Law* (Cambridge, Cambridge University Press, 2003), p. 1.

[62] M.-F. Lücker-Babel, 'The Non-Derogable Rights of the Child in the Light of the United Nations Convention on the Rights of the Child', in: D. Prémont, C. Stenersen and I. Oseredczuk (eds.), *Droits intangibles et états d'exception* (Brussels, Bruylant, 1996), p. 389.

is to assume that the CRC continues to apply during an armed conflict.[63] The very inclusion of an IHL provision—Article 38—in a human rights treaty—the CRC—proves the reconcilability of IHL and human rights. After all, both bodies of law have the same basic underpinning, the same etymological roots,[64] and according to some even the same future.[65]

1.2. Article 38 of the CRC

16. As stated above, this reconcilability finds a concrete reflection in Article 38 of the CRC. This article is structured according to a typical IHL scheme: its first paragraph contains a general provision on the applicability of IHL, the second and third paragraph deal with the protection of children from participation in hostilities or recruitment in the armed forces, and the fourth paragraph reminds the States Parties to protect the civilian population. Materially speaking, the article as a whole clearly covers IHL substance, which is reinforced by its explicit references to IHL and the terminology ('hostilities', 'recruiting', 'civilian population', ...) used. This seems to suggest that the terms contained in Article 38 of the CRC should be interpreted in line with their meaning under IHL.

17. However, formally speaking, this article is part of a human rights instrument and therefore monitored by a human rights body, namely the CRC Committee. The latter can indeed examine State compliance with IHL obligations.[66] This is in keeping with the tendency for UN human rights bodies—deemed appropriate for these purposes by scholars[67]—to deal with not only human rights but also IHL.[68] In so doing,[69] the CRC Committee has adopted a combatant-civilian transcending approach and speaks about armed conflict in terms of human rights.[70] Being the principal monitoring body of the CRC,

---

[63] J. Dhommeaux, 'Le rôle du Comité des droits de l'enfant dans le contrôle, l'interprétation et l'évolution de la Convention relative aux droits de l'enfant', in: K. Vasak, *Liber Amicorum: Les droits de l'homme à l'aube du XXIᵉ siècle* (Brussels, Bruylant, 1999), p. 557.

[64] Although the adjective 'humanitarian' concerns the contents of IHL norms and not the subjects bound by them—as opposed to the meaning of 'human' in the notion of 'human rights'. Y. Dinstein, 'Human Rights in Armed Conflict', in: T. Meron (ed.), *Human Rights in International Law: Legal and Policy Issues* (Oxford, Clarendon Press, 1984), p. 347.

[65] T. Meron, 'The Humanization of Humanitarian Law', *l.c.* (note 56), p. 239.

[66] R. Brett, 'Child soldiers: law and practice', *International Journal of Children's Rights* 4, No. 2, 1996, p. 116.

[67] F. Hampson, 'Using International Human Rights Machinery to Enforce the International Law of Armed Conflicts', *Revue de droit militaire et de droit de la guerre* 31, No. 2, p. 120.

[68] F. Kalshoven and L. Zegveld, *o.c.* (note 50), p. 200.

[69] D. O'Donnell, 'Trends in the Application of International Humanitarian Law by United Nations Human Rights Mechanisms', *International Review of the Red Cross*, No. 324, 1998, p. 481.

[70] *Cf. infra* No. 23.

the Committee's authority and competence to interpret the Convention should be upheld. Therefore, it seems that this Committee could play an important role in the reconciliation of IHL and human rights: by fitting in the IHL terminology and spirit into the human rights framework, both branches of public international law can be brought together closer than ever.

2. First Paragraph: A Safety Net Provision

2.1. Object: *Rules of IHL Applicable to States Parties in Armed Conflicts which are Relevant to the Child*

2.1.1. *Rules of IHL*

In theory: what can be understood under the term 'rules of IHL'?
18. The term 'IHL' is in fact relatively recent: it is not even mentioned in the 1949 Geneva Conventions.[71] Historically, the law applicable in armed conflicts, or so-called *ius in bello*, exclusively dealt with the regulation of the behaviour of belligerents (*i.e.* States, unless it concerned a case of 'recognition of belligerency')[72] in war and neutrality,[73] as codified in nine out of the thirteen 1907 Hague Conventions and the Regulations annexed to the Fourth Hague Convention.[74] This branch of law understandably became known as 'Hague Law'. Originally separately from this Hague Law, 'Geneva Law' was created, which was mostly laid down in the 1949 Geneva Conventions[75] and consisted of the rules on the protection of the person.[76] However, this traditional distinction between Hague Law and Geneva Law to a great extent became void with the adoption of the 1977 Additional Protocols to the 1949 Geneva Conventions: since that date, Geneva Law encompasses all the *ius in bello*, with the sole exception of the rules of neutrality and eco-

---

[71] Christopher Greenwood, 'Historical Development and Legal Basis', in: D. Fleck (ed.), *The Handbook of Humanitarian Law in Armed Conflicts* (Oxford, Oxford University Press, 1995), p. 9.
[72] I. Brownlie, *Principles of Public International Law* (Oxford, Oxford University Press, 2003), p. 63; H. Haug, *Humanity for All: The International Red Cross and Red Crescent Movement* (Henry Dunant Institute/Paul Haput, Geneva/Bern, 1993), p. 557.
[73] I. Detter, *The Law of War* (Cambridge, Cambridge University Press, 2000), p. 158.
[74] The Hague Rules on Aerial Warfare (reprinted in A. Roberts and R. Guelff, *Documents on the Laws of War* (Oxford, Oxford University Press, 2000), pp. 141–153) are not legally binding: the document is not a treaty and not all of the rules contained in it are considered customary international law.
[75] There is also a 1925 Geneva Convention, which was entirely taken over by the 1949 Geneva Conventions.
[76] I. Detter, *o.c.* (note 73), p. 158.

nomic warfare (and possibly the prohibition of arms *per se*, but not according to their uses or effects as these also fall under Geneva Law).[77]

The definition of 'IHL' used by the ICRC and mentioned *supra* in No. 11, perfectly matches this evolution. Although it would be possible to argue that the term 'IHL' only covers this Geneva Law—since this would be the only 'genuinely humanitarian' law, as opposed to the Hague Law regulating methods and means of combat—, excellent advocacy by the ICRC and eminent scholars like Jean Pictet[78] have effectuated a widely accepted agreement[79] on using the term 'IHL' for both Geneva and Hague Law. By broadening the scope of this term, attention is much more focused on the central issue of the treatment of the *individual*, whether civilian or military, thereby also contributing to the evolution of 'humanisation of humanitarian law' as described above.

19. Concretely, the following legally binding instruments are generally understood to fall under 'IHL': the four 1949 Geneva Conventions[80] and their 1977 Additional Protocols,[81] the 1907 Hague Conventions and the Hague Regulation as annexed to the Fourth 1907 Hague Convention,[82] the 1868 Saint Petersburg

---

[77] G. Abi-Saab, 'The specificities of humanitarian law', in: C. Swinarski (ed.), *Etudes et essais sur le droit international humanitaire et sur les principes de la Croix-Rouge en l'honneur de Jean Pictet* (Geneva, Comité international de la Croix-Rouge, 1984), p. 265.

[78] A. Eide, 'The laws of war and human rights—Differences and convergences', in: C. Swinarski (ed.), *o.c.* (note 44), p. 675.

[79] The term 'IHL' is used in the title and text of the 1977 Final Act of the diplomatic conference which concluded the 1977 Additional Protocols, the 1993 ICTY and 1994 ICTR Statutes, the 1994 San Remo Manual, and the 1997 Ottawa Convention: A. Roberts and R. Guelff, *o.c.* (note 74), p. 2.

[80] Convention (I) of 12 August 1949 for the Amelioration of the Condition of the Wounded and Sick in Armed Forces in the Field (GC1); Convention (II) of 12 August 1949 for the Amelioration of the Condition of Wounded, Sick and Shipwrecked Members of Armed Forces at Sea (GC2); Convention (III) of 12 August 1949 relative to the Treatment of Prisoners of War (GC3); Convention (IV) of 12 August 1949 relative to the Protection of Civilian Persons in Time of War (GC4).

[81] Protocol of 8 June 1977 Additional to the Geneva Conventions of 12 August 1949, and relating to the Protection of Victims of International Armed Conflicts (AP1); Protocol of 8 June 1977 Additional to the Geneva Conventions of 12 August 1949, and relating to the Protection of Victims of Non-International Armed Conflicts (AP2).

[82] Conventions of 18 October 1907: Convention (III) relative to the Opening of Hostilities; Convention (IV) respecting the Laws and Customs of War on Land and its annex: Regulations concerning the Laws and Customs of War on Land; Convention (V) respecting the Rights and Duties of Neutral Powers and Persons in Case of War on Land; Convention (VI) relating to the Status of Enemy Merchant Ships at the Outbreak of Hostilities; Convention (VII) relating to the Conversion of Merchant Ships into War-Ships; Convention (VIII) relative to the Laying of Automatic Submarine Contact Mines; Convention (IX) concerning Bombardment by Naval Forces in Time of War; Convention (X) for the Adaptation to Maritime Warfare of the Principles of the Geneva Convention; Convention (XI) relative to certain Restrictions

Declaration,[83] the 1899 Hague Declaration,[84] the 1925 Geneva Gas Protocol,[85] the London *Procès-Verbal*,[86] the 1954 Cultural Property Convention[87] and its 1999 Cultural Property Protocol,[88] the 1972 Biological Weapons Convention,[89] the ENMOD Convention,[90] the Conventional Weapons Convention[91] and its five Protocols,[92] and the 1997 Ottawa Convention.[93] Not legally binding but quite influential are the 1923 Hague Rules on Aerial Warfare and the 1994 San Remo Manual,[94] while the 1994 UN Safety Personnel Convention[95] does not belong to IHL *per se*, but is relevant as it provides for the inviolability of certain personnel during armed hostilities.[96] Also some case law particularly addressing issues related to IHL from the International Court of Justice (ICJ) is important for the interpretation of these provisions: the 1996 Advisory Opinion of the ICJ on the Legality of the Threat or Use of Nuclear Weapons,[97]

---

with regard to the Exercise of the Right of Capture in Naval War; Convention (XII) relative to the Creation of an International Prize Court; Convention (XIII) concerning the Rights and Duties of Neutral Powers in Naval War.

[83] Saint Petersburg Declaration of 11 December 1868 Renouncing the Use, in Times of War, and Explosive Projectiles under 400 grammes Weight.

[84] Hague Declaration of 29 July 1899 Concerning Expanding Bullets, so-called 'dum-dum bullets'.

[85] Geneva Protocol of 17 June 1925 for the Prohibition of the Use in War of Asphyxiating, Poisonous or Other Gases and of Bacteriological Methods of Warfare.

[86] London *Procès Verbal* of 6 November 1936 Concerning the Rules of Submarine Warfare.

[87] Hague Convention of 14 May 1954 for the Protection of Cultural Property in the Event of Armed Conflict.

[88] Second Hague Protocol to the Hague Convention of 1954 for the Protection of Cultural Property in the Event of Armed Conflict of 26 March 1999.

[89] Convention of 10 April 1972 on the Prohibition of the Development, Production and Stockpiling of Bacteriological (Biological) and Toxin Weapons and on their Destruction.

[90] Convention of 18 May 1977 on the Prohibition of Military or any other Hostile Use of Environmental Modification Techniques.

[91] Convention of 10 October 1980 on Prohibitions or Restrictions on the Use of Certain Conventional Weapons which May be Deemed to be Excessively Injurious or to Have Indiscriminate Effects.

[92] Protocol I of 10 October 1980 on Non-Detectable Fragments; Protocol II of 10 October 1980 and amended on 3 May 1996 on Prohibitions or Restrictions on the Use of Mines, Booby-Traps and Other Devices; Protocol III of 10 October 1980 on Prohibitions or Restrictions on the Use of Incendiary Weapons; Protocol IV of 13 October 1995 on Blinding Laser Weapons; Protocol V of 28 November 2003 on Explosive Remnants of War.

[93] Ottawa Convention of 18 September 1997 on the Prohibition of the Use, Stockpiling, Production and Transfer of Anti-Personnel Mines and on Their Destruction.

[94] 1994 San Remo Manual on International Law Applicable to Armed Conflicts at Sea, reprinted in: L. Doswald-Beck (ed.), *San Remo Manual on International Law Applicable to Armed Conflicts at Sea* (Cambridge, Cambridge University Press, 1995), pp. 5–44.

[95] UN Convention of 9 December 1994 on the Safety of United Nations and Associated Personnel.

[96] A. Roberts and R. Guelff, *o.c.* (note 74), p. 34.

[97] ICJ, Legality of the Threat or Use of Nuclear Weapons, Advisory Opinion, I.C.J. Reports, 1996, pp. 265–267.

for instance, discusses very important legal questions that are directly relevant to IHL.

20. Furthermore, there is a strong case for considering legal instruments related to international criminal tribunals or courts as also being part of 'rules of IHL'.[98] These would include the statutes of the Nuremberg Tribunal,[99] ICTY,[100] ICTR[101] and ICC[102] as legally binding instruments, and the judgements rendered by those tribunals or courts as secondary legal sources.[103] Given the fact that criminal proceedings fulfil an essential function in the enforcement of IHL, it seems logical to include these instruments in the interpretation of 'rules of IHL' as meant in Article 38 of the CRC.

Article 4(e) of the ICTY Statute, Article 2(e) of the ICTR Statute and Article 6(e) of the ICC Statute state that 'genocide', which falls within the material competence of the respective tribunals, means (*inter alia*) '*forcibly transferring children* of the group to another group, with intent to destroy, in whole or in part, a national, ethnical, racial or religious group'. Under Article 7§1(c) *juncto* Article 7§2(c) of the ICC Statute, the exercise of any or all of the powers attaching to the right of ownership over a person [including] the exercise of such power in the course of trafficking in persons, *in particular women and children*, amounts to 'enslavement', which is a crime against humanity when this is committed as part of a widespread or systematic attack directed against any civilian population, with knowledge of the attack. These articles are obviously pure applications of the obligation to protect children in armed conflicts, as laid down in Article 38 of the CRC.

Moreover, Articles 8§2(b)(xxvi) and 8§2(e)(vii) *juncto* Article 8§1 of the ICC Statute make it a war crime to *conscript or enlist children under the age of fifteen years* into the national armed forces or to use them to participate

---

[98] A. Roberts and R. Guelff, *o.c.* (note 74), p. 35.

[99] Charter of the Nuremberg International Military Tribunal, 8 August 1945.

[100] Statute of the International Criminal Tribunal for the Former Yugoslavia, adopted 25 May 1993 by Security Council Resolution S/RES/827 (1993), as amended by Security Council Resolutions 1166 (1998), 1329 (2000), 1411 (2002), 1431 (2002), and 1481 (2003).

[101] Statute of the International Criminal Tribunal for the Prosecution of Persons Responsible for Genocide and Other Serious Violations of IHL Committed in the Territory of Rwanda and Rwandan Citizens responsible for genocide and other such violations committed in the territory of neighbouring States, between 1 January 1994 and 31 December 1994, as amended by the Security Council acting under Chapter VII of the Charter of the United Nations.

[102] Rome Statute of the International Criminal Court of 17 July 1998 (UN Doc. A/CONF.183/9, 1998), corrected by procès-verbaux of 10 November 1998, 12 July 1999, 30 November 1999, 8 May 2000, 17 January 2001 and 16 January 2002, entered into force 1 July 2002.

[103] In the language of Article 38 of the Statute of the International Court of Justice of 26 June 1945, entered into force 24 October 1945 (ICJ Statute).

actively in hostilities, both in international and non-international armed conflicts. Especially these provisions are a clear-cut example of the intrinsic IHL character of these instruments.

21. But a State is not only bound by treaties: under Article 38 of the ICJ Statute, also customary international law is applicable to States. This is the case regardless whether a certain State is a party to treaties reflecting or evolving customary rules,[104] as was pointed to by the ICJ in the North Sea Continental Shelf Case.[105] It can be said that, broadly speaking, the four 1949 Geneva Conventions, Hague Convention IV and the Regulations annexed thereto, the Genocide Convention, and the Nuremberg Charter are considered customary international law.[106] The recent and comprehensive ICRC study on customary international humanitarian law is fully dedicated to the question of the customary international law status of IHL rules.[107] Recently, the Special Court for Sierra Leone has ruled that the recruitment of children under the age of 15 in hostilities is a war crime under customary international law.[108]

22. In theory, all the instruments mentioned above are part of the 'rules of IHL' referred to in Article 38§1 of the CRC. A closer look at the practice of the CRC Committee, however, reveals a much narrower vision on the content of the notion 'IHL', as will be discussed now.

The CRC Committee practice: a narrow understanding of the term 'IHL'
23. First of all, the CRC Committee seems to prefer not to mention any IHL instruments in its concluding observations—not even core ones such as the 1949 Geneva Conventions. The ICC Statute apparently does not deserve the status of being part of 'rules of IHL' either. Furthermore, notwithstanding the explicit requirement taken up in the CRC Committee's General Guidelines for Periodic Reports[109] for States Parties to indicate in their Periodic

---

[104] A. D'Amato (ed.), *International Law Anthology* (Cincinnati, Anderson Publishing Company, 1994), p. 52.

[105] ICJ, Federal Republic of Germany v. Denmark; Federal Republic of Germany v. Netherlands, Merits, Judgement, 20 February 1969 (I.C.J. Reports, 1969, p. 4) et seq., para. 71.

[106] Report of the Secretary-General pursuant to paragraph 2 of Security Council resolution 808 (1993), with which he introduced the Statute of the ICTY, and which was unanimously approved by the Security Council (Resolution 827 (1993)). Referred to by the ICJ in the Legality of Nuclear Weapons Advisory Opinion. *Cf.* W. Kälin (ed.), *Human Rights in Times of Occupation: The Case of* Kuwait (Bern, Stämpfli, 1994), p. 20.

[107] J.-M. Henckaerts and L. Doswald-Beck (eds.), *Customary International Humanitarian Law* (Cambridge, Cambridge University Press, 2005), 3 volumes.

[108] Special Court for Sierra Leone, *Prosecutor v. Sam Hinga Norman*, 31 May 2004, Case No. SCSL-2004-14-AR72(E), para. 53.

[109] CRC Committee, *General Guidelines for Periodic Reports* (UN Doc. CRC/C/58, 1996).

Reports[110] the 'relevant IHL applicable to the State',[111] the CRC Committee only refers to 'violations of provisions of IHL' in general, without going into further detail.[112]

Secondly, the Committee has adopted an indirect approach. In its concluding observations on the Democratic Republic of the Congo,[113] it explicitly involves the UN report on the illegal exploitation of natural resources and other forms of wealth of the Democratic Republic of the Congo.[114] The CRC Committee considers the substance of IHL only via the reference to external sources, and even here without going into much detail.

Finally, the CRC Committee's narrow understanding of what constitute 'rules of IHL' is proved by the link consistently made by the CRC Committee between IHL and human rights. The obligation that States have under IHL to permit relief actions by neutral States or humanitarian organisations if the civilian population of a party to the conflict is inadequately supplied with indispensable goods,[115] for instance, is referred to in terms of the right of the child to water and food,[116] which are obviously human rights notions.[117] In doing so, the CRC Committee also considers a typical IHL issue such as the use of child soldiers as a violation of human rights.[118] To a certain extent this practice of not using IHL as an independent body of law renders the reference in Article 38 of the CRC to IHL useless.

24. Although it is regrettable that the CRC Committee does not seem to find itself an apt forum to extensively monitor States Parties compliance with IHL via Article 38 of the CRC, it must be reiterated here that in accordance with the saving clause contained in Article 41 of the CRC, States Parties are under the obligation to provide the broadest possible protection of the

---

[110] Under Article 44(b) of the CRC, States Parties undertake to submit to the Committee, through the Secretary-General of the United Nations, reports on the implementation of the Convention every five years after the submission of the Initial Report.

[111] Para. 123.

[112] *E.g.* CRC Committee, *Concluding Observations: Russian Federation* (UN Doc. CRC/C/15/Add.110, 1999), para. 56; *Burundi* (UN Doc. CRC/C/15/Add.133, 2000), para. 72; *Democratic Republic of the Congo* (UN Doc. CRC/C/15/Add.153, 2001), para. 6.

[113] CRC Committee, *Concluding Observations: Democratic Republic of the Congo* (UN Doc. CRC/C/15/Add.153, 2001), para. 6.

[114] Final report of the Panel of Experts on the Illegal Exploitation of Natural Resources and Other Forms of Wealth of the Democratic Republic of the Congo (UN Doc. S/2002/1146, 2002).

[115] Article 23 of the GC4; Article 70 of the AP1.

[116] Article 6 of the CRC.

[117] CRC Committee, *Concluding Observations: Sudan* (UN Doc. CRC/C/15/Add.190, 2002), para. 59.

[118] CRC Committee, *Concluding Observations: Democratic Republic of the Congo* (UN Doc. CRC/C/15/Add.153, 2001), para. 64.

rights of the child applicable to them. Concretely this means that the rest of Article 38 only applies to the extent that States are not bound by another, stronger obligation. Thus, this first paragraph of Article 38 of the CRC functions as a kind of 'residuary provision' or 'safety net': via this provision it is possible to invoke a whole body of law that is strictly speaking not part of the CRC.

2.1.2. Rules Applicable in Armed Conflicts

25. Originally, *ius in bello* was only deemed applicable if there was a formal 'state of war', which was only achieved if, and only if, one of the parties to the conflict had made it clear that it regarded itself as being in a state of war.[119] The linguistic shift from 'war' to 'armed conflict' signals the different vision being upheld nowadays: in spite of the ambiguous wording of common Article 2§1 of the 1949 Geneva Conventions, it is now well established that any factual armed conflict makes IHL applicable, regardless of the question whether a formal declaration of the state of war has been made or not.[120] By only requiring the event of 'armed conflicts', Article 38 of the CRC unambiguously opts for this solution.

26. Although the term 'armed conflict' is used throughout the Geneva Conventions and their Additional Protocols, they do not give a definition of this concept.[121] According to the ICTY, 'an armed conflict exists whenever there is a resort to armed force between States or protracted armed violence between governmental authorities and organized armed groups or between such groups within a State'.[122] Within IHL, a traditional distinction is made between international armed conflicts and non-international ones.[123] Taking a look at the definition given by the ICTY, it seems that the distinction is still relevant. This is not just so for the definition of an armed conflict, but also for the application of IHL,[124] and via the reference to 'rules

---

[119] C. Greenwood, 'Scope of Application of Humanitarian Law', in: D. Fleck (ed.), *o.c.* (note 71), p. 41.

[120] *Ibid.*, p. 43.

[121] H. Haug, *o.c.* (note 72), pp. 510–511.

[122] ICTY Appeals Chamber, *Prosecutor v. Dusko Tadić*, 2 October 1995, para. 70.

[123] Comité international de la Croix-Rouge, 'Protocole facultative à la Convention des Nations Unies relative aux droits de l'enfant concernant l'implication d'enfants dans les conflits armés', *Revue internationale de la Croix-Rouge* 80, No. 829, 1998, p. 124.

[124] *Ibid.*

of IHL' in Article 38§1 of the CRC also for the application of Article 38 of the CRC itself: depending on this international or non-international character of a conflict, different substantive rules are applicable in several different situations.

27. Under IHL, a conflict is international if it takes place between two or more States, involving action by the armed forces,[125] if it concerns a partial or total occupation, even if the occupation meets with no armed resistance, and if Article 1§4 of AP1 is applicable. The latter is the case if the conflict takes place in the territory of one State but involves the exercise of the right of self-determination and is directed against colonial domination, alien occupation or a racist regime. According to the *Commentaries on the Geneva Conventions*, it does not matter how long or how deadly a dispute is for a qualification as an international armed conflict.[126] In those three situations, the law of international armed conflicts applies, which basically includes the full range and detail of IHL.[127]

28. For non-international armed conflicts, the notion of 'armed conflict' is harder to define.[128] A first kind of non-international armed conflict triggers the applicability of AP2: the conflict takes place in the territory of one State but does not fall under Article 1§4 of AP1. In this case, AP2 is applicable under the following conditions:[129] first the conflict must be between the forces of the State and dissident armed forces, secondly the latter must be in such control over part of the territory as to enable them to carry out sustained and concerted military operations, thirdly they must be under responsible command and able to implement AP2, and finally, as will be discussed below,[130] internal 'disturbances and tensions' are excluded.[131] Consequently, the threshold to trigger the applicability of AP2 is much stricter than the one laid down in Article 2 of AP1 for international armed conflicts. Furthermore, AP2 does not contain the same level of protection or detailed regulations as AP1 does.[132]

---

[125] Common Article 2 of the GC.

[126] J. Pictet (ed.), *Commentary on the Geneva Convention relative to the Protection of Civilian Persons in Time of War* (Geneva, ICRC, 1956), p. 20.

[127] *Cf. supra* No. 19 for a listing of IHL instruments.

[128] Comité international de la Croix-Rouge, 'Protocole facultative à la Convention des Nations Unies relative aux droits de l'enfant concernant l'implication d'enfants dans les conflits armés', *l.c.* (note 123), p. 125.

[129] Article 1§1 of the AP2.

[130] *Cf. infra* No. 30.

[131] Article 1§2 of the AP2.

[132] *E.g.* the non-existence of 'grave breaches' (triggering universal jurisdiction) in AP2. *Cf.*

29. Luckily enough, non-international armed conflicts are not only regulated by AP2. In any 'armed conflict not of an international character', common Article 3 of the 1949 Geneva Conventions is applicable. Compared to AP2, this 'mini-treaty within a treaty'[133] accords even fewer guarantees to the individuals to which it applies—which is of course still better than nothing. At least Article 3 is generally considered to be customary international law,[134] thereby even binding States that are not a party to the Geneva Conventions, for the rules contained in this article were 'recognized as essential in all civilized countries, and embodied in the municipal law of the States in question, long before the Geneva Conventions were signed'.[135] This is why the ICRC is in favour of giving Article 3 as wide a scope as possible, including with regard to the definition of an armed conflict.[136]

30. Conflict situations such as internal disturbances or riots are not explicitly excluded by Article 38 of the CRC, but under current IHL as outlined above, the use of the term 'armed conflict' implies the exclusion of those lower-intensity conflicts.[137] This points to a very unfortunate gap in the scale of protection of individuals: the existence of a 'public emergency threatening the life of the nation', which results in the derogation of a major part of international human rights law, is not linked in any way[138] to the existence of an armed conflict, which would trigger the applicability of IHL. This gap, in honour of its 'finder' commonly referred to as 'the Meron gap',[139] occurs whenever a State declares the state of emergency[140] without there

---

L.C. Green, *The Contemporary Law of Armed Conflict* (Manchester, Manchester University Press, 2000), p. 61.

[133] E. Chadwick, '"Rights" and International Humanitarian Law', in: C. Gearty and A. Tomkins (eds.), *o.c.* (note 60), p. 578.

[134] *Cf. supra* No. 21.

[135] J. Pictet, *o.c.* (note 126), p. 36.

[136] Comité international de la Croix-Rouge, 'Protocole facultatif à la Convention des Nations Unies relative aux droits de l'enfant concernant l'implication d'enfants dans les conflits armés', *l.c.* (note 123), p. 125.

[137] C. Greenwood, 'Scope of Application of Humanitarian Law', in: D. Fleck (ed.), *l.c.* (note 71), p. 47.

[138] F.J. Hampson, Legal Protection Afforded to Children under International Humanitarian Law: Report for the Study on the Impact of Armed Conflict on Children, available at <http://www.essex.ac.uk/armedcon/international/comment/Text/paper002.htm>, Subsection 2.2.1.

[139] T. Meron, 'On the Inadequate Reach of Humanitarian and Human Rights Law and the Need for a New Instrument, *American Journal of International Law* 77, July, p. 603 *et seq.*

[140] Which can be done under strict conditions only (*Cf. supra* Chapter II) but is still up to the State.

being enough violence so as to qualify the situation as an armed conflict. Notwithstanding some attempts to fill the gap later,[141] it is still there.

The African Children's Charter can be called a progressive actor in this field. Quite revolutionary it explicitly *includes* the applicability of its Article 22 to 'tensions and strife'.[142] Also the CRC Committee has been seduced to consider rules of IHL to be applicable notwithstanding the circumstance that the needed threshold of violence was not reached: in its concluding observations on the 2000 report of the Central African Republic,[143] the Committee 'recommends that the State party protect children from the effects of armed conflict *or other strife* within the State party'. So it seems that the CRC Committee does not adhere to a very strict interpretation of what constitutes an armed conflict.

31. Furthermore, it is positive to note that Article 38 of the CRC is applicable to *all* types of armed conflict. As mentioned above, contemporary armed conflicts are hard to squeeze into the categories of 'international', 'high-intensity non-international' (AP2), or 'low-intensity non-international' (common Article 3 of the Geneva Conventions): set aside the risk of manipulation of the thresholds by States,[144] more and more conflicts are genuinely difficult to categorize. The conflict in the former Yugoslavia shows how armed conflicts can change both temporally and geographically. For this reason, and—more fundamentally—because it is hard to understand 'why protect civilians from belligerent violence [. . .] when two sovereign States are engaged in war, and yet refrain from [. . .] providing the same protection when armed violence has erupted "only" within the territory of a sovereign State',[145] it is laudable that the ICTY has expressed itself in favour of the recent tendency to blur the different thresholds of applicability. This tendency is shown by some other sources that do not make the distinction between international and non-international armed conflicts anymore, such as many military manuals,[146] the UN Secretary-General Bulletin on the obser-

---

[141] *E.g.* the drafting of the 'Turku Declaration' (Declaration of Minimum Humanitarian Standards of 2 December 1990, Annex to UN Doc. E/CN.4/Sub.2/1991/55, 1991), a non-binding instrument drafted by legal experts. It was meant to become a legally binding declaration at one point, but almost 15 years later, it does not seem to be getting anywhere.

[142] *Cf. supra* Chapter II.

[143] CRC Committee, *Concluding Observations: Central African Republic* (UN Doc. CRC/C/15/Add.138, 2000), para. 83, emphasis added.

[144] T. Meron, 'The Humanization of Humanitarian Law', *l.c.* (note 56), pp. 260–261.

[145] ICTY Appeals Chamber, *Prosecutor v. Dusko Tadić*, 2 October 1995, para. 97.

[146] T. Meron, 'The Humanization of Humanitarian Law', *l.c.* (note 56), p. 261.

vance by UN forces of IHL,[147] and recent instruments concerning weapons like the 1996 Amended Protocol II to the Conventional Weapons Convention and the 1997 Ottawa Convention.

32. At least by not explicitly mentioning different qualifications of armed conflicts but instead using the single formulation of 'armed conflicts', Article 38 of the CRC in principle follows this new tendency within IHL to transcend the traditional distinction between international and non-international armed conflicts. Moreover, the CRC Committee's occasional interpretation of the term 'armed conflicts' discloses a willingness to make Article 38 applicable to conflicts that actually do not meet the high threshold of violence traditionally required. In this respect, Article 38§1 of the CRC can therefore be labelled a progressive provision.

2.1.3. Rules Applicable to States Parties

33. Under general public international law, a State is bound by treaties that it is a party to. Combined with the saving clause, the ratified instrument that provides the strongest protection of the rights of the child is applicable. This has some interesting consequences with regard to children and armed conflicts: the two[148] States in the world that are not a party to the Geneva Conventions nor their Additional Protocols (Marshall Islands and Nauru)[149] are a party to the ICC Statute, thereby making the conscription and enlistment of children under the age of 15 years and their use in hostilities a war crime. Several States that are not a party to the Additional Protocols did ratify ILO Convention 182[150] (Fiji, Indonesia, Iran, Iraq, Japan, Malaysia, Morocco, Nepal, Pakistan, Papua New Guinea, Singapore, Sri Lanka, Sudan, Thailand, Turkey, and USA), which obliges States Parties to 'take immediate and effective measures to secure the prohibition and elimination of the worst forms of child labour as a matter of urgency',[151] protecting all persons under the age of 18[152] from (*inter alia*) 'all forms of slavery or practices similar to slavery, such as [. . .] forced or compulsory labour,

---

[147] Secretary-General's Bulletin: Observance by United Nations Forces of IHL of 6 August 1999, entered into force 12 August 1999 (UN Doc. ST/SGB/1999/13, 1999).
[148] Timor Leste became a party to the Geneva Conventions and the Additional Protocols on 13 December 2002.
[149] As of 4 August 2004.
[150] ILO Convention 182 concerning the Prohibition and Immediate Action for the Elimination of the Worst Forms of Child Labour of 17 June 1999, entered into force 19 November 2000.
[151] Article 1 of the ILO Convention 182.
[152] Article 2 of the ILO Convention 182.

including forced or compulsory recruitment of children for use in armed conflict'.[153]

34. The cited provisions from both the ICC Statute and ILO Convention 182 apply to all types of armed conflicts. This means that they are especially relevant to those States that have not ratified AP2, relating to non-international armed conflicts. At this moment this is the case for Angola (which is, as mentioned, also a party to the African Children's Charter), Mexico and Viet Nam. Also the Child Soldiers Protocol does not make the distinction between international and non-international armed conflicts, which makes it particularly important with regard to Andorra, Azerbaijan, Morocco and the USA, not being parties to the Additional Protocols. Finally, comparing is also helpful in the opposite situation: the Philippines, not being a party to AP1, has ratified ILO Convention 182, thereby prohibiting the forcible or compulsory recruitment of persons under the age of 18 in all types of armed conflicts.

35. In short, a State Party to the CRC is bound by all rules of IHL that have customary law status and by all legally binding instruments concerning IHL to which it is a party, whereby the instrument providing the strongest protection in terms of children's rights is applicable by priority.

2.1.4. *Rules which Are Relevant to the Child*

36. The CRC drafting history clearly puts forward that the phrase 'which are relevant to the child' applies to the 'rules of IHL', and not to 'armed conflicts', as it would not make sense to assume that there are armed conflicts which are not relevant to the child: '[...] armed conflicts normally have severe impacts on the population in general, on the provision of services, including food, health and education, and on the infrastructure, and also tend to affect adults who are relevant to the child, such as fathers and brothers'.[154] The self-evident impact of armed conflicts on every child has always been of great concern to the CRC Committee.[155] The key issue of defining a 'child' will be discussed in Subsection 2.2.

---

[153] Article 3 of the ILO Convention 182.
[154] R. Brett, 'Child soldiers: law and practice', *l.c.* (note 66), p.116.
[155] *E.g. Concluding Observations: El Salvador* (UN Doc. CRC/C/15/Add.9, 1993), paras. 11 and 14; *Sudan* (UN Doc. CRC/C/15/Add.6, 1993), para. 9; *Sri Lanka* (UN Doc. CRC/C/15/Add.40, 1995), paras. 24 and 44; *Yugoslavia* (UN Doc. CRC/C/15/Add.49, 1996), paras. 3 and 5; *Kuwait* (UN Doc. CRC/C/15/Add.96, 1998), para. 8; *Armenia* (UN Doc. CRC/C/15/Add.119, 2000), para. 7; *Lebanon* (UN Doc. CRC/C/15/Add.169, 2002), para. 50; *United Kingdom* (UN Doc. CRC/C/15/Add.288, 2002), para. 53.

37. Before dealing with the rules contained in the Geneva Conventions and their Additional Protocols, the core documents of IHL, it can be recalled that child-related provisions are taken up in the above-mentioned IHL and human rights instruments. As described, the Statutes of the ICTY, ICTR and ICC contain specific provisions on the enslavement, genocide and recruitment of children, while ILO Convention 182 includes the forced or compulsory recruitment of children in its notion of the 'worst forms of child labour'. The relevance of Article 22 of the African Children's Charter has also been discussed, and the Child Soldiers Protocol is dealt with in a separate contribution.

38. The rules of IHL relevant to the child that are part of the Geneva Conventions and their Additional Protocols will be analysed in more detail in Sections 3 to 6, but broadly speaking there are two categories of protection in those instruments: on the one hand, there are rules regulating the treatment of child *civilians*, and on the other hand, there are those regulating the treatment of child *combatants*. With regard to the first category, child civilians benefit from the 'general protection' in their capacity as civilians and from a 'special protection' in their capacity as children. A key feature of this last subcategory is the protection from participation in hostilities and from recruitment, which will be discussed in Sections 3 and 4/5 respectively dealing with Article 38§2 of the CRC and Article 38§3 of the CRC. The extent of general protection and of the remainder of special protection given to child civilians will be the topic of Section 6 dealing with Article 38§4 of the CRC. The treatment of child combatants will be dealt with below.[156]

2.2. Right Holder: *the Child*

39. In what way the term 'child' mentioned in Article 38§1 of the CRC is to be interpreted, is not an easy question. In light of the conclusion reached in the Introduction to this Chapter, all notions brought up in this article should be interpreted within the framework of IHL, taking a look at the sources inherent to this body of law. The drafters of the Geneva Conventions had taken the conscious decision not to fix one maximum age limit to define the term 'child'.[157] This resulted in the creation of different definitions of the 'child' which was called by Géraldine Van Bueren the 'six ages of child-

---

[156] *Cf. infra* No. 43–44.
[157] C. Pilloud, J. De Preux, Y. Sandoz *et al.*, *Commentaire des protocoles additionnels du 8 juin 1977 aux Conventions de Genève du 12 août 1949* (The Hague/Geneva, Nijhoff/Comité International de la Croix-Rouge, 1986), p. 923.

hood':[158] in IHL, the word 'child' can refer to new-born babies, infants, people under 7, people under 12, people under 15, and people between the ages of 15 and 18. Each age leads to a different treatment or status.

40. On the other hand, Article 1 of the CRC states that *'[f]or the purposes of the present Convention*, a child means every human being below the age of 18 years unless under the law applicable to the child, majority is attained earlier'.[159] Based on the fact that other paragraphs of Article 38 of the CRC explicitly indicate deviating age limits, it would be logical to conclude that it is an overall valid definition, to be used in the whole of the CRC—including its Article 38. According to Article 38 *juncto* Article 1 of the CRC, States Parties are bound by all rules of IHL relevant to the category of under-18s, thereby not following the approach taken by IHL to make age-related distinctions within that category.

41. Concerning the definition of the minimum age of the child, it could be argued that—potentially contrary to Article 1 of the CRC—the special protection under IHL already starts as from the conception. Since there are some provisions relating to the treatment of expectant mothers (*e.g.* on the establishment of safety and hospital zones),[160] the drafters of the Geneva Conventions and other relevant instruments might have wanted to protect expectant mothers not only on account of themselves but also of their foetus—and in any case the result is the same. This reasoning is, moreover, fully reconcilable with the *Commentary* to the Fourth Geneva Convention.[161] The CRC, on the other hand, does not explicitly mention the minimum age of the child in its first Article. As no consensus could be reached between those in favour of conception and those in favour of birth as the childhood starting point,[162] the whole issue was shifted to the legally non-binding Preamble of the CRC[163] and left open in Article 1 of the CRC. For the purposes of interpreting Article 38§1 of the CRC, this entails the possibility to understand the word 'child' in a way that includes the unborn 'child'.

---

[158] G. Van Bueren, *The International Law of the Child* (The Hague, Martinus Nijhoff Publishers, 1998), p. 333.

[159] (emphasis added)

[160] Article 14 of the GC4.

[161] J. Pictet, *La Convention de Genève relative à la protection des personnes civiles en temps de guerre: Commentaire* (Geneva, Comité International de la Croix-Rouge, 1956), p. 135.

[162] S. Detrick (ed.), *The United Nations Convention on the Rights of the Child: A Guide to the "Travaux Préparatoires"* (Dordrecht/Boston/London, Martinus Nijhoff Publishers, 1992), p. 26.

[163] Preamble para. 10 reads: 'Bearing in mind that, as indicated in the Declaration of the Rights of the Child, "the child, by reason of his physical and mental immaturity, needs special safeguards and care, including appropriate legal protection, *before as well as after birth*", [...]' (emphasis added).

42. A particular problem arises when defining who is a child within the framework of Article 38 of the CRC. It appears that the second, third and fourth paragraph of Article 38 of the CRC exclusively deal with the legal framework applicable to child *civilians*. Admittedly it might look different if one does not consider the rules regarding the participation in hostilities or recruitment to be rules regulating the treatment of *civilians* but instead of *combatants*—an opinion shared by most scholars writing on Article 38 of the CRC, who indeed differentiate between paragraphs 2 and 3 under the heading 'participation in hostilities and recruitment' on the one hand, and on the other hand paragraph 4 under the heading 'protection and care of civilians'. A strong case could be made, however, to view the rules on participation in hostilities and recruitment as being an integral part of the rules on the treatment of child civilians, for it is the child civilian—and not the child combatant—who is protected by those rules. Obviously, the child combatant does not benefit very much from the protection from participation in hostilities or recruitment: he or she is already fighting, he or she is already a member of the armed forces.

43. Nevertheless, child combatants should not be forgotten when defining who is a child according to Article 38 of the CRC. Its scope does include that group of children as well.

First of all, since its paragraphs 2 and 3 prohibit the participation and recruitment of under-15s in hostilities, they create the obligation for States Parties to demobilize those child combatants.[164] States violating public international law are responsible for the cessation of the violation and the granting of a reparation.[165] Therefore, unlawfully recruited child soldiers have to be demobilized, even regardless of the absence of an explicit obligation hereto in Article 39 of the CRC.

Moreover, as explained above,[166] Article 38§1 of the CRC serves as a safety net provision: through this provision, all States Parties are bound to instruments of IHL that they are a party to. This means that the second category of protection—the rules regulating the treatment of child combatants—is, being part of the rules of IHL relevant to the child, fully applicable to the States Parties, albeit to the extent that the latter are a party to those rules. Under IHL, captured child combatants are entitled to the extensive and

---

[164] However, this is generally considered to fall under Article 39 of the CRC and not Article 38 paras. 2–3 of the CRC.
[165] I. Brownlie, *o.c.* (note 72), p. 445; M.N. Shaw, *o.c.* (note 47), pp. 714 and 716.
[166] *Cf. supra* No. 24.

strong protection granted to prisoners of war,[167] notwithstanding the possibility to qualify child combatants as 'unlawful combatants'.[168] This protection includes important guarantees such as the right to humane treatment.[169] 'Child war criminals' also receive a specific treatment with a view to their young age.[170] However, the situation of child combatants who are not captured is not explicitly regulated under IHL.

Finally, the CRC as a whole is applicable to *all* children. The human rights system does not differentiate between 'combatants' and 'civilians', as IHL does. This would go against the concept of human rights itself.[171] Therefore, also child combatants are entitled to the rights laid down in the CRC. In general, the Committee indeed predominantly speaks of the rights of 'children' in armed conflict, without making a further distinction.[172] When commenting on the traumatic effect of armed conflicts on children, it sometimes specifies that the group of 'child victims' includes child combatants.[173] And now and then, the Committee even explicitly declares certain rights such as the right to mental integrity[174] and the right not to be subjected to sexual exploitation[175] applicable to child combatants. Hence, the CRC Committee has chosen to allow to adopt the general human rights approach not to differentiate between child civilians and child combatants.

---

[167] Article 77 of the AP1. *Cf.* also *CRC Committee, Concluding Observations: Sri Lanka* (UN Doc. CRC/C/15/Add.40, 1995), para. 24 and F. Bouchet-Saulnier, *The Practical Guide to Humanitarian Law* (Lanham, Rowman & Littlefield Publishers, 2002), p. 38.

[168] C. Pilloud, J. De Preux, Y. Sandoz *et al., o.c.* (note 157), p. 925.

[169] See in general: Third Geneva Convention.

[170] *E.g.* Article 7 of the Statute of the Special Court for Sierra Leone. Compare A. Crawford, 'Child War Criminals: Is it possible to prevent child soldiers being held criminally responsible for war crimes whilst also satisfying the right to justice in Sierra Leone?', in: *European master's degree in human rights and democratisation, Awarded theses of the academic year 2000/2001* (Venice, Marsilio, 2001), pp. 133–198 to C. Reis, 'Trying the Future, Avenging the Past: The implications of prosecuting children for participation in internal armed conflict', *Columbia Human Rights Law Review* 28, No. 4, pp. 629–655.

[171] *Cf. supra* No. 10.

[172] *E.g.* CRC Committee, *Concluding Observations: Cambodia* (UN Doc. CRC/C/15/Add.128, 2000), para. 48; *Colombia* (UN Doc. CRC/C/15/Add.137, 2000), para. 11; *Sierra Leone* (UN Doc. CRC/C/15/Add.116, 2000), paras. 44 and 72; *Sudan* (UN Doc. CRC/C/15/Add.190, 2002), para. 35.

[173] *E.g.* CRC Committee, *Concluding Observations: Sierra Leone* (UN Doc. CRC/C/15/Add.116, 2000), para. 71; *Liberia* (UN Doc. CRC/C/15/Add.236, 2004), para. 58; *Myanmar* (UN Doc. CRC/C/15/Add.237, 2004), para. 67.

[174] CRC Committee, *Concluding Observations: United Kingdom* (UN Doc. CRC/C/15/Add.188, 2002), para. 53.

[175] CRC Committee, *Concluding Observations: Sierra Leone* (UN Doc. CRC/C/15/Add.116, 2000), para. 87.

2.3. State Party Obligations:
To Undertake to Respect and to Ensure Respect for

44. The phrase 'to undertake to respect and to ensure respect for' is clearly based on and quite literally taken from Article 1 common to the four Geneva Conventions and the First Additional Protocol, which reads 'The High Contracting Parties undertake to respect and to ensure respect for the present Convention [*respectively 'this Protocol'*] in all circumstances'. Within IHL, a lot of literature is dedicated to the interpretation of the scope of this formulation; and in the course of time, it has grown its own very specific meaning.

45. Naturally, it would have been possible to follow common human rights language, containing a similar phrase in Article 2§1 of the CCPR: 'Each State Party to the present Covenant *undertakes to respect and to ensure* to all individuals within its territory and subject to its jurisdiction *the rights recognized in the present Covenant*, without distinction of any kind [. . .]'.[176] This formulation, too, has grown its own meaning, which to a certain extent corresponds to its IHL counterpart. As explained by Manfred Nowak, this entails both a negative and a positive duty for States Parties. The duty to respect indicates the *negative character* of civil and political rights, obliging States Parties to *refrain* from restricting the exercise of these rights where such is not expressly allowed,[177] while the duty to 'ensure rights' is a *positive* one, obliging States Parties to take positive *steps* to give effect to the rights.[178] This view, forwarding the two dimensions of State Party obligations, has now become prevalent[179] and is also used to interpret Article 38§1 of the CRC.

46. Although this view is, as stated above, to a certain extent transplantable to IHL,[180] the latter attaches a much broader meaning to the phrase 'to respect and to ensure respect'. The different wording used—'to ensure [rights]' versus 'to ensure *respect* for [rights]'—already suggests that the formulation in IHL should be interpreted differently.

---

[176] (emphasis added)
[177] M. Nowak, *U.N. Covenant on Civil and Political Rights: CCPR Commentary* (Kehl/Strasbourg/Arlington, N.P. Engel, 1993), p. 36.
[178] M. Nowak, *o.c.* (note 177), p. 37.
[179] S. Detrick, *o.c.* (note 6), p. 68.
[180] R. Brett, 'Child soldiers: law and practice', *l.c.* (note 66), p. 116.

2.3.1. *To Undertake to Respect*

47. If accepting the autonomous meaning of this phrase in IHL, one could wonder what the added value could be of an article merely confirming that the legal instrument *in casu* is to be respected by the States Parties: are not States by definition obliged to respect a legal instrument that they are a Party to,[181] especially bearing in mind Article 26 of the Vienna Convention on the Law of Treaties?[182] Of course they are, but in light of the historical origin of this formulation, it is still understandable why the drafters of the Geneva Conventions—and decades later those of the CRC—have chosen to explicitly oblige States Parties to undertake to respect the Convention (or Protocol) in question.

48. Until 1929, when the two 1929 Geneva Conventions were adopted, both of which contain the obligation to respect the Convention in all circumstances, *ius in bello* only came into play if all parties to the conflict were a party to the laws of war. This means that whenever one of the belligerents was not a party to this law, the latter was simply not applicable, as was stated in the *si omnes* clause which was part of all relevant instruments of the laws of war.[183] By revolutionarily obliging States Parties to respect the Convention in all circumstances, it was made clear that this type of legal instruments is not just a contract based on reciprocity[184] (also called the *tu quoque* principle).[185] The 1949 Geneva Conventions and further IHL instruments are all interpreted in a similar way: regardless of the 'enemy' being bound by or even complying with IHL, States Parties must respect this law—as confirmed in Article 60§5 of the Vienna Convention on the Law of Treaties[186] and in the ICTY Zupreskic case.[187]

---

[181] L. Condorelli and L. Boisson de Chazournes, 'Quelques remarques à propos de l'obligation des Etats de "respecter et faire respecter" le droit international humanitaire "en toutes circonstances"', in: C. Swinarski (ed.), *Etudes et essais sur le droit international humanitaire et sur les principes de la Croix-Rouge en l'honneur de Jean Pictet* (Geneva, Comité international de la Croix-Rouge, 1984), p. 17.

[182] Vienna Convention of 22 May 1969 on the Law of Treaties, entered into force 27 January 1980.

[184] L. Condorelli and L. Boisson de Chazournes, *l.c.* (note 181), p. 19.

[185] J. Pictet, *o.c.* (note 161), p. 24.

[186] L. Boisson de Chazournes and L. Condorelli, 'Common Article 1 of the Geneva Conventions revisited: Protecting collective interests', *International Review of the Red Cross* 82, No. 837, 2000, p. 75.

[186] Article 60§5 of the Vienna Convention on the Law of Treaties makes an exception to the principle of reciprocity for 'provisions relating to the protection of the human person contained in treaties of a humanitarian character'.

[187] ICTY Trial Chamber, *The Prosecutor v. Zoran Kupreskic and others*, Judgement, 14 January

49. Nowadays, the duty to 'respect' is also supposed to entail the applicability of this duty to armed forces[188] of a State fighting abroad. This extra-territorial applicability also occurs in human rights treaties.[189]

50. Notwithstanding all these elements attached to the core of this duty to 'respect', the CRC Committee has not really elaborated on any of those.[190] In fact, it seems to prefer using the phrase 'to ensure respect' instead, even to describe obligations that normally would fall under the duty to 'respect',[191] both in the human rights interpretation (positive State Party obligations) and in the IHL one (no reciprocity, extraterritorial application). Given the fact that in accordance with the latter interpretation it is of course very well possible to consider the duty to 'respect' as a part of the duty to 'ensure respect for', this 'omission' from the part of the CRC Committee does not necessarily diminish the extent of State Party obligations.

2.3.2. To Undertake to Ensure Respect

51. Contrary to the duty to 'respect', the obligation to 'ensure respect for' is not a common phrase in the language of international human rights law. A quick glance at the French official text immediately clarifies the difference between *s'engager à faire respecter* (to undertake to ensure respect) and *s'engager à garantir les droits* (to undertake to ensure the rights), the former being an obligation to make sure that 'others' respect the law, as opposed to the second phrase which is an obligation for oneself to make sure that the rights provided for in the law are guaranteed. Within IHL, however, 'to ensure respect for' has become one of the most significant provisions of the Geneva Conventions and the First Additional Protocol.[192]

52. There seems to be a tendency in the direction of a very far-stretching interpretation. Not only are States Parties thus not allowed to leave the detailed implementation of IHL solely to the armed forces, they also have

---

2000, Case No IT-95–16-T, para. 517—not contested in appeal: ICTY Appeals Chamber, *The Prosecutor v. Zoran Kupreskic and others*, Judgement, 23 October 2001, Case No IT-95–16.

[188] This is also true for other persons who are not a member of the official armed forces of a State but who are acting under the command and control of that State, irrespective of their nationality: ICTY Appeals Chamber, *The Prosecutor v. Dusko Tadic*, Judgement, 15 July 1999, Case No IT-94–1, para. 145.

[189] *E.g.* Article 2 of the CCPR.

[190] *E.g.* CRC Committee, *Concluding Observations: Burundi* (UN Doc. CRC/C/15/Add.133, 2000), para. 72.

[191] *E.g.* CRC Committee, *Concluding Observations: Armenia* (UN Doc. CRC/C/15/Add.119, 2000), para. 49.

[192] L. Boisson de Chazournes and L. Condorelli, *l.c.* (note 185), p. 85.

to ensure that the humanitarian principles underlying IHL are applied universally.[193]

53. One way of achieving the universal application of IHL, as obliged by the duty to 'ensure respect for', is the regulation of the behaviour of non-State actors.[194] As those cannot become a party to the CRC, it is still up to the States Parties to ensure respect by other, non-State, actors for IHL.[195] The CRC Committee is of the opinion that these non-State actors include 'armed groups',[196] 'rebel forces',[197] and even 'paramilitary groups'[198] and 'private companies'.[199] Even if there is *de facto* control by non-State actors, the CRC Committee 'emphasizes the full responsibility of the State Party', thereby 'inviting all other parties to respect child rights within the area under their control'.[200] By directly calling upon non-State actors to comply with Article 38 of the CRC,[201] the CRC Committee has decided to apply the general IHL understanding that also non-State actors are bound by IHL. This is rather remarkable, given the denial of any such obligation for non-State actors under human rights law.[202] Thus, searching for the highest protection, the CRC Committee seems to prefer to blur the frontiers between both bodies of public international law on this point.

54. Moreover, the duty to 'ensure respect for', obliges States Parties to take legal and other measures in peacetime necessary for the application of IHL whenever needed. One of these measures that necessarily have to be taken beforehand, *i.e.* in peacetime,[203] is the establishment by law of the minimum age for recruitment. Sweden, not involved in any armed conflict whatsoever, for instance, caused concern to the CRC Committee because its

---

[193] G. Van Bueren, *o.c.* (note 158), p. 330.

[194] S. Detrick, *o.c.* (note 6), p. 651.

[195] *Cf.* the more general discussion on the horizontal effects of the CRC: S. Detrick, *o.c.* (note 6), p. 31.

[196] CRC Committee, *Concluding Observations: Myanmar* (UN Doc. CRC/C/15/Add.237, 2004), para. 66; *Rwanda* (UN Doc. CRC/C/15/Add.234, 2004), para. 62.

[197] *E.g.* CRC Committee, *Concluding Observations: Comoros* (UN Doc. CRC/C/15/Add.141, 2000), para. 45; *Lebanon* (UN Doc. CRC/C/15/Add.169, 2002), para. 50.

[198] *E.g.* CRC Committee, *Concluding Observations: Colombia* (UN Doc. CRC/C/15/Add.137, 2000), paras. 34 and 54; *Indonesia* (UN Doc. CRC/C/15/Add.223, 2004), para. 71(d).

[199] *E.g.* CRC Committee, *Concluding Observations: Democratic Republic of the Congo* (UN Doc. CRC/C/15/Add.153, 2001), para. 6.

[200] CRC Committee, *Concluding Observations: Sudan* (UN Doc. CRC/C/15/Add.190, 2002), para. 6.

[201] *E.g.* CRC Committee, *Concluding Observations: Israel* (UN Doc. CRC/C/15/Add.195, 2002), para. 32.

[202] I. Brownlie, *o.c.* (note 72), p. 65; M.N. Shaw, *o.c.* (note 47), p. 232.

[203] J. Pictet, *o.c.* (note 161), p. 24.

legislation allowed children under 18 in its Home Guard Defence.[204] Other measures concern the advancement of the dissemination of IHL.[205] This is sporadically present in the CRC Committee's concluding observations, stressing the need for training programmes on the rights of the child, as well as in the areas of international human rights and humanitarian law,[206] in accordance with Article 29§1(b) of the CRC.

55. Another major part of the duty to 'ensure respect for' is the national implementation of penal obligations under IHL: as prescribed by the four 1949 Geneva Conventions, States Parties 'undertake to enact any legislation necessary to provide effective penal sanctions for persons committing, or ordering to be committed, any of the grave breaches [. . .]'.[207] Grave breaches being exhaustively[208] enumerated violations of IHL of a particularly grave nature, also 'lesser' violations are to be suppressed in national systems.[209] In this respect it is interesting to note that the principle of universal jurisdiction, as laid down in the 1949 Geneva Conventions,[210] is also considered to fall within the obligation to 'ensure respect for'.[211] Up to date, the CRC Committee has primarily gone into the fight against impunity in general: it consistently recommends or approves of the establishment of judicial[212] and extra-judicial[213] mechanisms to deal with gross human rights and IHL violations in the past, every now and then referring to the importance of making sanctions publicly known as a means of dissemination and pre-

---

[204] CRC Committee, *Concluding Observations: Sweden* (UN Doc. CRC/C/15/Add.2, 1993), paras. 8 and 11.

[205] L. Boisson de Chazournes and L. Condorelli, 'Common Article 1 of the Geneva Conventions revisited: Protecting collective interests', *l.c.* (note 185), p. 71.

[206] *E.g.* CRC Committee, *Concluding Observations: Iraq* (UN Doc. CRC/C/15/Add.94, 1998), para. 14.

[207] Article 49 para. 1 of the GC1; Article 50 para. 1 of the GC2; Article 129 para. 1 of the GC3; Article 146 para. 1 of the GC4.

[208] Article 50 of the GC1; Article 51 of the GC2; Article 130 of the GC3; Article 147 of the GC4; Article 85 of the AP1.

[209] Article 49 para. 3 of the GC1; Article 50 para. 3 of the GC2; Article 129 para. 3 of the GC3; Article 146 para. 3 of the GC4.

[210] Article 49 para. 2 of the GC1; Article 50 para. 2 of the GC2; Article 129 para. 2 of the GC3; Article 146 para. 2 of the GC4.

[211] J. Pictet, *o.c.* (note 161), p. 24; L. Boisson de Chazournes and L. Condorelli, 'Common Article 1 of the Geneva Conventions revisited: Protecting collective interests', *l.c.* (note 185), p. 77.

[212] *E.g.* CRC Committee, *Concluding Observations: Croatia* (UN Doc. CRC/C/15/Add.52, 1996), para. 9.

[213] *E.g.* CRC Committee, *Concluding Observations: Sierra Leone* (UN Doc. CRC/C/15/Add.116, 2000), para. 45.

vention for the future.[214] It also refers to individual criminal responsibility,[215] though without ever raising the possibility of implementing universal jurisdiction. This is rather unfortunate, given the emergence of a new conviction, as put by the ICTY: '[. . .] these norms of IHL do not pose synallagmatic obligations, *i.e.* obligations of a State vis-à-vis another State. Rather [. . .] they lay down obligations towards the international community as a whole, with the consequence that each and every member of the international community has a "legal interest" in their observance and consequently a legal entitlement to demand respect for such obligations'.[216]

56. This finally leads to another, somewhat controversial, dimension of the duty to 'ensure respect for': this duty entails the obligation for every State Party to make sure that other States (also) respect IHL. The CRC Committee interprets this part of the duty in a strictly financial way, as it only seems to be concerned with the financial co-operation of States, and this without pointing to States' possibility to support other States who need the resources. Instead, it only recommends States in need to look for assistance,[217] thereby neglecting States' positive duty to co-operate under Article 38§1 of the CRC. Still, it is possible to interpret the duty to 'ensure respect for' in a much broader way: based on this obligation, the High Contracting Parties to the Fourth Geneva Convention have convened some meetings to discuss the situation of the Israeli-occupied Palestinian territories, feeling the need to show Israel it was clearly failing to fulfil its obligations under this Geneva Convention.[218] This is a very interesting and significant precedent, especially bearing in mind the expressed intention of the High Contracting Parties to convene more such meetings.[219]

---

[214] *E.g.* CRC Committee, *Concluding Observations: Ethiopia* (UN Doc. CRC/C/15/Add.67, 1997), para. 31.

[215] *E.g.* CRC Committee, *Concluding Observations: Uganda* (UN Doc. CRC/C/15/Add.80, 1997), para. 34.

[216] ICTY, *The Prosecutor v. Zoran Kupreskic and others*, Trial Chamber, Judgement, 14 January 2000, Case No 11-95-16-T, para. 519.

[217] *E.g.* CRC Committee, *Concluding Observations: Myanmar* (UN Doc. CRC/C/15/Add.69, 1997), para. 31; *Iraq* (UN Doc. CRC/C/15/Add.94, 1998), para. 14; *Chad* (UN Doc. CRC/C/15/Add.107, 1999), para. 35; *Comoros* (UN Doc. CRC/C/15/Add.141, 2000), para. 46; *Guinea-Bissau* (UN Doc. CRC/C/15/Add.177, 2002), para. 49(d).

[218] Statement by the Conference of High Contracting Parties to the Fourth Geneva Convention, 15 July 1999 and Declaration by the Conference of High Contracting Parties to the Fourth Geneva Convention, 5 December 2001, available at <http://www.eda.admin.ch/eda/e/home/foreign/hupol/4gc.html>.

[219] L. Boisson de Chazournes and L. Condorelli, *l.c.* (note 185), p. 80.

57. Article 38§1 of the CRC, therefore, has great potential in terms of monitoring compliance with the provisions of this article and the rest of IHL. In some fields, the CRC Committee seems to have tried to make up for the flaws left by the disagreeing drafters of the CRC.[220] In other, likewise important, fields, however, the CRC Committee apparently has chosen to remain silent, which is highly regrettable in light of the renewed spirit blown into this essential paragraph via the recent tendencies in IHL.

3. *Second Paragraph: Protection from Hostilities*

3.1. Object: *Direct Participation in Hostilities*

58. 'Hostilities' are considered in the *Commentaries to the Additional Protocols* to cover the 'acts of war which are intended by their nature or their purpose to hit specifically the personnel and the "materiel" of the armed forces of the adverse Party', including 'preparations for combat and the return from combat'. Of course there is some margin of appreciation: to restrict the concept of 'hostilities' to active military operations would be too narrow, while extending it to the entire war effort would be too broad, as in modern warfare the whole population participates in the war effort to some extent, albeit indirectly.[221] Still, there does not seem to be any disagreement on the meaning of the notion.[222]

59. 'Direct participation' to hostilities, on the contrary, is much harder to define. One uncontested element of this concept is the interpretation that the 'participation' is to be assessed objectively, *i.e.* regardless of the will of the child in question. Apparently, the majority of the drafters of Article 38§2 of the CRC found that the insertion of 'against his or her will' would be 'contrary to the spirit of the Convention.[223] This is the more interesting as it entirely contrasts with the approach taken on the 'recruitment' definition.[224]

---

[220] S. Bischhoff, *The UN Convention on the Rights of the Child: A Comparative Study* (Amsterdam, Vrije Universiteit Amsterdam, 1999), p. 231.

[221] Y. Sandoz, C. Swinarski and B. Zimmermans (eds.), *Commentary on the Additional Protocols of 8 June 1977* (Geneva, International Committee of the Red Cross, 1987), p. 516.

[222] *E.g.* it was not an issue raised in the Working Groups drafting the CRC: S. Detrick (ed.), *o.c.* (note 162), pp. 502–517. *Cf.* the discussion in Comité international de la Croix-Rouge, 'Protocole facultative à la Convention des Nations Unies relative aux droits de l'enfant concernant l'implication d'enfants dans les conflits armés', *l.c.* (note 123), p. 126.

[223] S. Detrick (ed.), *o.c.* (note 162), p. 506.

[224] *Cf. infra* Subsection 4.1.

60. According to the above-mentioned *Commentaries*, the notion of 'direct participation' implies a direct causal relationship between the activity engaged in and the harm done to the enemy at the time and the place where the activity takes place.[225] It could be argued that this definition simply shifts the problem from defining 'direct participation' to defining 'direct causal link': 'it is not clear whether a messenger [. . .] or deliverer of ammunition could be included'.[226] Examples of 'indirect participation' enumerated in literature are the transport of arms and munitions along the front lines of a battle,[227] the search for and transmission of military information,[228] and acts of sabotage.[229] Obviously, these 'indirect participation' acts can be as dangerous as 'direct participation',[230] both for the child in question and for other children, for there is a real risk that any participation of some children in hostilities casts suspicion on and creates danger for all children.[231]

61. Therefore it is highly unfortunate that Article 38§2 of the CRC apparently allows children under the age of 15 years to take such an 'indirect part' in hostilities. Many delegations belonging to the Working Groups drafting this article had expressed to be in favour of the deletion of the word 'direct',[232] but in the end, the adoption of the third paragraph[233] was considered to render the prevention of 15- to 18-year olds taking *any* part in hostilities while they could be legitimately recruited, unrealistic.[234] In any case, also at the legal level these individuals would be lawful subjects of attack under IHL, so it would be impossible to ensure they would never be involved in hostilities.[235] There was also a small yet strong opposition against improving standards already fixed in *e.g.* Article 77§2 of AP1[236] because a Working Group was not seen as an appropriate forum to revise Article 77 of AP1 which was the result of lengthy debates at the highest level.[237]

---

[225] Y. Sandoz, C. Swinarski and B. Zimmermans (eds.), *o.c.* (note 221), p. 516.
[226] F. Hampson, *o.c.* (note 138), Subsection 4.5.1.
[227] G. Van Bueren, *o.c.* (note 158), p. 334.
[228] C. Pilloud, J. De Preux, Y. Sandoz *et al.*, *o.c.* (note 157), p. 925.
[229] C. Pilloud, J. De Preux, Y. Sandoz *et al.*, *o.c.* (note 157), p. 1400.
[230] G. Van Bueren, *o.c.* (note 158), p. 334.
[231] A. Sheppard, 'Child soldiers: Is the optional protocol evidence of an emerging "straight-18" consensus?', *The International Journal of Children's Rights* 8, No. 1, 2000, p. 51.
[232] S. Detrick (ed.), *o.c.* (note 162), p. 509.
[233] *Cf. infra* Sections 4 and 5.
[234] S. Detrick (ed.), *o.c.* (note 162), p. 513.
[235] M.J. Dennis, 'Newly Adopted Protocols to the Convention on the Rights of the Child', *American Journal of International Law*, 2000, p. 791.
[236] S. Detrick, *o.c.* (note 6), p. 653.
[237] S. Detrick (ed.), *o.c.* (note 162), p. 513.

62. It is true that the ICRC's proposal, only containing 'participation in hostilities', was modified by the States that drafted Article 77§2 of AP1 into 'direct participation in hostilities'. Although it would be logical to conclude that indirect participation is allowed, the authors of the *Commentaries to the Additional Protocols*, one of the most authoritative sources for the interpretation of IHL, maintain that the intention still is to keep all children away from all hostilities, in every way.[238]

63. Nevertheless, as was already well-known at the time of drafting of the CRC[239] and has been continuously raised by many scholars ever since,[240] this language—while indeed merely confirming the law applicable in international armed conflicts—actually lowers the standard set for high-intensity non-international armed conflicts: Article 4§3(c) of AP2 prohibits children under the age of 15 years to 'take part in hostilities', thereby excluding both direct and indirect participation. It is one of the rare provisions offering a higher level of protection for non-international armed conflicts compared to the law applicable in international armed conflicts. So in fact it should have been cherished, in accordance with Resolution IX adopted at the 25th International Conference of the Red Cross,[241] which specifically recalled that the level of protection in the CRC (then under consideration) should be at least the same as that accorded by the Geneva Conventions and the two Additional Protocols.[242] Yet '[i]t did not work out quite that way':[243] the blunt wording of Article 38§2 pushes the standard of protection downward for children in non-international armed conflicts, instead of upward for children in international armed conflicts.

64. The Child Soldiers Protocol is in a way reminiscent of this inconsistent duality of allowing indirect participation in international armed conflicts on the one hand, while prohibiting any participation in non-international armed conflicts on the other hand. A combined reading of its Articles 1 and 4 inevitably leads to the conclusion that under the Child Soldiers Protocol—

---

[238] M. Bothe, K.J. Partsch and W.A. Solf, *New Rules for Victims of Armed Conflict* (Martinus Nijhoff Publishers, The Hague/Boston/London, 1982), p. 477; C. Pilloud, J. De Preux, Y. Sandoz *et al.*, *o.c.* (note 157), p. 925.

[239] S. Detrick (ed.), *o.c.* (note 162), p. 509.

[240] S. Bischhoff, *o.c.* (note 220), p. 230; S. Detrick, *o.c.* (note 6), p. 656; G. Van Bueren, *o.c.* (note 158), p. 334.

[241] Articles 2–3 of the Resolution No IX of the International Conference of the Red Cross, reprinted in *International Review of the Red Cross*, No. 256, 1986, p. 340.

[242] I. Cohn and G.S. Goodwin-Gill, *Child Soldiers: The Role of Children in Armed Conflict* (Oxford, Clarendon Press, 1994), p. 68.

[243] I. Cohn and G.S. Goodwin-Gill, *o.c.* (note 242), p. 69.

which was originally drafted to make up for the flaws left by the creation of the CRC[244]—State governments can allow children to take an indirect part in hostilities if the latter are a member of the State armed forces, while this is prohibited if they belong to non-State armed groups. Thus, even in non-international armed conflicts, the Child Soldiers Protocol permits children to take an indirect part in hostilities, which (the definition of the child set aside) also lowers the standard set in AP2. As non-State actors were not involved in the negotiations during the drafting of the Protocol, they did not have any say in the creation of the final result. Therefore it is obvious that one of the key problems is to encourage non-State actors to adhere to rules that are being imposed on them in an entirely top-down mode, and more-over treat them in a less favourable way compared to the official armed forces.[245]

65. Another legal instrument dealing with the participation of children in hostilities is the ICC Statute. The adoption of this Statute constituted one of the most significant steps in the worldwide fight against impunity. Since neither the Additional Protocols, nor the CRC provide for compulsorily penal sanctions regarding the participation of children in hostilities,[246] it is the ICC Statute which, for the very first time, criminalizes the use of children under the age of 15 years to participate actively in hostilities, in both international and non-international armed conflicts.[247] By using the formulation 'active participation', it might be argued that the ICC language is broader than that of the CRC or its Child Soldiers Protocol, which would represent an advance in IHL.[248] Under current IHL, however, 'active' participation is not automatically interpreted in a broader way. The *Commentaries to the Geneva Conventions* seem to equate 'actively participating' (as it is mentioned in Common Article 3 of the Geneva Conventions)[249] to 'fighting', which would narrow the scope of the prohibited type of participation down to

---

[244] S. Detrick, *o.c.* (note 162), p. 658.

[245] R. Stohl, 'Children in conflict: assessing the Optional Protocol', *Conflict, Security & Development* 2, No. 2, 2002, p. 138.

[246] J.T. Holmes, 'The Protection of Children's Rights in the Statute of the International Criminal Court', in: M. Politi and G. Nesi (eds.), *The Rome Statute of the International Criminal Court: A Challenge to Impunity* (Ashgate, Aldershot, 2001), p. 120.

[247] Articles 8 para. 2(b)(xxvi) and 8 para. 2(e)(vii) of the ICC Statute.

[248] D. Helle, 'Optional Protocol on the involvement of children in armed conflict to the Convention on the Rights of the Child', *International Review of the Red Cross*, No. 839, 2000, p. 802; J.T. Holmes, 'The Protection of Children's Rights in the Statute of the International Criminal Court', in: M. Politi and G. Nesi (eds.), *l.c.* (note 246), p. 121.

[249] J. Pictet, *Commentary on the Geneva Conventions* (Geneva, International Committee of the Red Cross, 1956), p. 53 (GC1), pp. 35–36 (GC2), p. 39 (GC3), p. 38 (GC4).

actual fighting, and thereby considerably broaden the scope of permitted types of indirect participation. In its Akayesu judgement, the ICTR has taken the view that 'active' and 'direct' participation are the same.[250] Yet it should be emphasized that it remains for the ICC itself to determine the exact meaning of this provision and its relation to other related provisions in the Additional Protocols and the CRC.[251]

66. The African Children's Charter, finally, follows the provisions as laid down in Article 38§2 of the CRC by prohibiting only the direct participation of children in hostilities.[252] As explained before, the global assessment of Article 22 of the African Children's Charter is a positive one. But, with a view to the emphases a regional human rights instrument can put on certain issues of particular importance to the region, it is very unfortunate that the AU has not chosen to prohibit *all* types of participation by children. According to the *International Coalition to Stop the Use of Child Soldiers*, an undoubtedly very influential coalition consisting of non-governmental organisations in nearly 40 countries around the world, the African continent has the sad honour of having the greatest number of children taking part in hostilities.[253] This actually confirms the common image most people have when thinking about 'the child soldier': a black boy with empty eyes and a big gun. Yet, generally ignored in literature and law dealing with children and armed conflicts,[254] there are also many *girls* who participate in hostilities.[255] In the first place, likewise generally ignored, girls are used as combatants.[256] A little bit more well-known, is the horror of girls being the 'wife' of the commanders. But next to this activity they also have a significant role in 'other supporting activities' that do not receive any media attention,[257]

---

[250] ICTR, *Prosecutor v. Jean-Paul Akayesu*, Judgement, Case No ICTR-96-4–T, para. 629.

[251] J.T. Holmes, 'The Protection of Children's Rights in the Statute of the International Criminal Court', in: M. Politi and G. Nesi (eds.), *l.c.* (note 246), p. 121.

[252] Article 22 para. 2 of the African Children's Charter.

[253] International Coalition to Stop the Use of Child Soldiers, *Child Soldiers Global Report* (Coalition to Stop the Use of Child Soldiers, London, 2001), p. 29. *Cf.* also F. Bugnion, 'Les enfants soldats, le droit international humanitaire et la Charte africaine des droits et du bien-être de l'enfant', *Revue Africaine de Droit International et Comparé*, No. 2, 2000, p. 265.

[254] M. Utas, 'Agency of Victims: Young Women in the Liberian Civil War', reprinted in F. De Boeck, *Anthropology of Children and Youth* (Leuven, Acco, 2002), p. 108. The otherwise very comprehensive study done by Ilene Cohn and Guy S. Goodwin-Gill, for instance, does not mention girls whatsoever . . .: *cf.* I. Cohn and G.S. Goodwin-Gill, *o.c.* (note 242).

[255] International Coalition to Stop the Use of Child Soldiers, *o.c.* (note 253), p. 21.

[256] Susan McKay, 'The Effects of Armed Conflict on Girls and Women', *Peace and Conflict: Journal of Peace Psychology* 4, 1998, p. 381.

[257] F. Grünfeld, 'Child Soldiers', in: J.C.M. Willems (ed.), *Developmental and Autonomy Rights of Children: Empowering Children, Caregivers and Communities* (Antwerp/Oxford/New York, Intersentia, 2002), p. 275.

such as cooking, cleaning, and carrying goods[258]—all of which fall under the 'indirect participation in hostilities'. By allowing this form of participation, many girls are forgotten. In this regard it should be pointed out that the African Children's Charter, unfortunately enough, does not contain a provision similar to Article 39 of the CRC, on the demobilisation and rehabilitation of children who were involved in armed conflict[259]—while Article 39 of the CRC, unfortunately enough, does not touch upon a gender approach.[260]

67. Given the above-mentioned flaws in the protection of children from participation in hostilities, it is laudable to note the CRC Committee's way of handling Article 38§2 in this respect. The CRC Committee in fact has adopted a 'straight-18' approach, whereby a minimum of 18 years is adopted for all ways in which one can become a member of the armed forces and all forms of participation in armed conflict,[261] which includes the prohibition of indirect participation. This is first of all expressed in its concluding observations, in which the CRC Committee explicitly claims to be concerned about the participation of children in Burundi, 'either as soldiers, or as helpers in camps or in the obtaining of information'[262] and at the massive participation of children in armed forces in Sierra Leone, 'either as combatants or in other roles'.[263] It has also strongly urged Israel 'to take immediate and all necessary measures to ensure that children [. . .] do not participate in the conflict',[264] implicitly omitting the condition of 'direct participation' as fixed in the Article 38§2 of the CRC. Moreover, the CRC Committee has adopted a General Recommendation on Children in Armed Conflict,[265] recalling 'the fundamental importance of raising the age of all forms of recruitment of children into the armed forces to eighteen years and the *prohibition of their involvement in hostilities*'.[266] The only regrettable element is the fact that CRC Committee does not systematically take up the gender angle when

---

[258] I. Vermeire, 'Meisjes in oorlog', in: B. Horemans and E. Vervliet (eds.), *Kindsoldaten. Laat ze niet schieten* (Brussel, Wereldwijd Mediahuis, 2002), p. 74.

[259] D. Olowu, 'Protection children's rights in Africa: A critique of the African Children's Charter on the Rights and Welfare of the Child', *l.c.* (note 10), p. 132.

[260] D. Mazurana and S. McKay, 'Child soldiers: What about the girls?', *Bulletin of the Atomic Scientists* 57, No. 5, 2002, p. 30.

[261] A. Sheppard, 'Child Soldiers', *l.c.* (note 231), p. 39.

[262] CRC Committee, *Concluding Observations: Burundi* (UN Doc. CRC/C/15/Add.133, 2000), para. 71.

[263] CRC Committee, *Concluding Observations: Sierra Leone* (UN Doc. CRC/C/15/Add.116, 2000), para. 26.

[264] CRC Committee, *Concluding Observations: Israel* (UN Doc. CRC/C/15/Add.1950, 2002), para. 32(b).

[265] CRC/C/80, 19th Session, September 1998.

[266] (emphasis added)

discussing the impact of armed conflict on children. It merely seems to do this in connection with the problem of sexual exploitation by armed persons, 'particularly with regard to girls'.[267] Recently, however, the Committee, has begun to dedicate special attention to gender when recommending the social reintegration of demobilized child soldiers.[268]

3.2. Right Holder: *Persons who Have Not Attained the Age of Fifteen Years*

68. This 'straight-18' approach taken by the CRC Committee and other actors active in the field of children's rights such as the *International Coalition to Stop the Use of Child Soldiers* can be seen as a reaction to the way in which the language of Article 38 of the CRC, *inter alia* regarding the minimum legal age for participation in hostilities and recruitment, was fixed at the time of drafting. The least one could say is that the Chairman's quest for a consensus in a Working Group consisting of delegations totally disagreeing among each other jeopardized an article that could have been a real advancement of the realization of children's rights.[269] The fact that the age limit has been fixed now at 15 years is the more odd, knowing that there were hardly any delegations from States in which children are more considered in terms of agency than of passivity.[270]

69. Regardless of the specific age at which one can be allowed to take a direct part in hostilities, there is always a pragmatic problem: often it is simply impossible to find out or prove one's age as some States—contrary to their obligation under Article 7 of the CRC—still do not have a compulsory birth registration system.[271] Sometimes identification cards are not issued until one's 18th birthday, or they are destroyed in the fighting.[272] It is therefore extremely hard to check age,[273] resulting by the way in diffi-

---

[267] CRC Committee, *Concluding Observations: Sierra Leone* (UN Doc. CRC/C/15/Add.116, 2000), para. 87.

[268] CRC Committee, *Concluding Observations: Liberia* (UN Doc. CRC/C/15/Add.236, 2004), para. 59; *Rwanda* (UN Doc. CRC/C/15/Add.234, 2004), para. 63. *Cf.* also CRC Committee, *General Discussion Day: The Girl Child* (UN Doc. CRC/C/38, 1995), para. 296, where the CRC Committee touches upon the situation of the girl child in armed conflicts in a very brief way.

[269] S. Detrick (ed.), *o.c.* (note 162), pp. 514–516.

[270] *Ibid.*, 24.

[271] I. Cohn and G.S. Goodwin-Gill, *o.c.* (note 242), p. 24.

[272] *Ibid.*

[273] Nevertheless, the CRC Committee keeps using age as the criterion, as this does not leave any room for interpretation. The Zambian legislation setting the minimum age for

culties in gathering the disaggregated information always requested[274] by the CRC Committee under Article 44 of the CRC and its General Guidelines regarding the submission of both initial[275] and periodic[276] reports.

70. As stated before, the CRC Committee tends to recommend States Parties to set the legal minimum age for recruitment and involvement in hostilities at 18 years.[277] This fits within the general policy of the CRC Committee to systematically recommend all States Parties to ratify the Child Soldiers Protocol, which is supposed to ban the direct participation of children under the age of 18 years.[278] Sometimes it also refers to the African Children's Charter, which, as explained above, contains an absolute definition of the child ('a child means every human being below the age of 18 years'),[279] resulting in an absolute prohibition of the participation of persons who have not attained the age of 18 years in hostilities.[280]

71. Nevertheless, the use of children between the ages of 15 and 18 years does not lead to criminal responsibility under the ICC Statute, and the measures that States are supposed to take under both AP1[281] and the CRC are

---

voluntary recruitment at 'the apparent age of 18 years' is therefore considered to be too arbitrary: CRC Committee, *Concluding Observations: Zambia* (UN Doc. CRC/C/15/Add.206, 2003), paras. 61–61.

[274] *E.g.* CRC Committee, *Concluding Observations: Yemen* (UN Doc. CRC/C/15/Add.47, 1996), para. 19; CRC Committee, *Concluding Observations: India* (UN Doc. CRC/C/15/Add.115, 2000), paras. 16–17.

[275] CRC Committee, *General guidelines regarding the form and content of initial reports to be submitted by States Parties under article 44, paragraph 1(a), of the Convention* (UN Doc. CRC/C/5, 1991), para. 7.

[276] CRC Committee, *General guidelines for periodic reports* (UN Doc. CRC/C/58, 1996), para. 7.

[277] *E.g.* CRC Committee, *Concluding Observations: Israel* (UN Doc. CRC/C/15/Add.195, 2002), para. 32(b) : 'The Committee strongly urges the State party and all relevant non-State actors: [. . .] to take immediate and all necessary measures to ensure that children are not recruited and do not participate in the conflict', by not defining 'children' implicitly setting eighteen as the minimum age. *Cf.* also CRC Committee, *Concluding Observations: Libyan Arab Jamahiriya* (UN Doc. CRC/C/15/Add.209, 2003), para. 21: '[t]he Committee is concerned that [. . .] although the age of compulsory recruitment into the armed forces is 18 years, article 1 of Mobilization Act No. 21 of 1991 allows for persons of 17 years to, among other things, engage in combat' and CRC Committee, *Concluding Observations: Cyprus* (UN Doc. CRC/C/15/Add.205, 2003), para. 57; *Solomon Islands* (UN Doc. CRC/C/15/Add.208, 2003), paras. 50(a) and 51(a); *Papua New Guinea* (UN Doc. CRC/C/15/Add.229, 2004), para. 56.

[278] Articles 1 and 4 of the Child Soldiers Protocol.

[279] Article 2 of the African Children's Charter.

[280] CRC Committee, *Concluding Observations: Sierra Leone* (UN Doc. CRC/C/15/Add.116, 2000), para. 73, prohibiting recruitment not only by the State but also 'any armed force or group', because of which this also falls under the 'participation in hostilities' as laid down in Article 38 para. 2 of the CRC.

[281] Article 86 of the AP1.

limited to children who have not attained the age of 15 years. Still, though the 'straight-18' approach is not criminally enforceable under current international law, the ICC Statute did establish for the first time the possible prosecution of violations taken place in the course of all types of non-international armed conflicts.[282] Neither common Article 3 of the Geneva Conventions nor AP2 provides for the penal suppression of breaches, whereas the ICC Statute does.

3.3. State Party Obligations: *To Take All Feasible Measures to Ensure*

72. States Parties to the CRC have to *take all feasible measures to ensure* that no one under the age of 15 years directly participates in hostilities. This obligation, which does not occur in international human rights language,[283] sounds rather weak, especially bearing in mind the original intention of many delegations involved in the drafting process to oblige States Parties to take all *necessary* measures to ensure this non-involvement of children.[284] Moreover, while this formulation coincides with the language used in Article 77§2 of AP1, it once again lowers the standard set in Article 4§3(c) of AP2, of which the wording is absolute ('children who have not attained the age of fifteen years shall neither be recruited in the armed forces or groups nor allowed to take part in hostilities').[285] Yet as a positive note can be remarked that States that are a party to both the CRC and AP2 are of course required to comply with AP2 in accordance with Article 41 of the CRC, while States that are only a party to the CRC at least are under *some* obligation to take measures in this field.

73. Although it is clear that the obligation to take 'feasible' measures is weaker than one to take 'necessary' measures, the latter being laid down in the African Children's Charter,[286] it is not so clear what exactly is to be understood under 'feasible'. Obviously it includes an element of practicality, as can already be seen when taking a look at the official French text ('*Les Etats parties prennent toutes les mesures possibles dans la pratique*') and the *Commentaries to the Additional Protocols* ('it should be understood as meaning

---

[282] Article 8 para. 2(e)(vii) of the ICC Statute.
[283] *Cf.* CCPR, CESCR, CEDAW, CERD, rest of CRC.
[284] S. Detrick (ed.), *o.c.* (note 162), p. 512.
[285] G. Van Bueren, *o.c.* (note 158), p. 334.
[286] Article 22 para. 2 of the African Children's Charter. This Charter thus offers the highest level of protection, which is in the spirit of the ICRC's recommendations: M.T. Dutli, 'Captured child combatants', *International Review of the Red Cross* 278, 1990, p. 421.

"capable of being done, accomplished or carried out, possible or practicable").[287] Still it could be argued that this language is deliberately rather vague to allow national armed forces to determine what is meant by 'feasible' measures[288]—where the limit naturally should be the States Parties obligation to 'ensure respect for rules of IHL'.[289]

74. The *Commentaries to the Additional Protocols* give some exemplary tips on the scope of the obligation 'to take all feasible measures'. To begin with, while excluding the automatic refusal of voluntary participation, for which reason 'necessary' was replaced by 'feasible' in the first place,[290] States are still under the obligation to be 'conscious of the heavy responsibility they are assuming' when accepting this voluntary participation.[291] Thus they should 'give them the appropriate instruction on handling weapons, the conduct of combatants and respect for the laws and customs of war'.[292] In practice, however, this obligation is often not complied with, as most children who are involved in hostilities—in the already rather exceptional case they get any instruction or training—are mainly brainwashed by, for instance, having to memorize biographies of local heroes.[293]

75. In line with the CRC Committee's General Guidelines for Periodic Reports, States Parties are explicitly requested to provide information on the measures adopted pursuant to Article 38§2 of the CRC, including of a 'legislative, administrative and educational nature', to ensure that persons who have not attained the age of 15 years do not take a direct part in hostilities.[294] The Guidelines also request States Parties to indicate the 'criteria used to assess the feasibility of measures adopted',[295] but it seems this has only to be done with regard to the measures taken pursuant to Article 38§4 of the CRC on the protection of the civilian population. In spite of these Guidelines, the CRC Committee's concluding observations mostly just confirm that the Committee is concerned if children are involved in hostilities, without indicating whether the State Party in question has failed to fulfil its duties under Article 38§2 (*e.g.* 'The Committee further urges the State

[287] Y. Sandoz, C. Swinarski and B. Zimmermans (eds.), *o.c.* (note 221), p. 895.
[288] R. Stohl, 'Children in conflict: assessing the Optional Protocol', *l.c.* (note 245), p. 138.
[289] *Cf. supra* Subsection 2.3.2.
[290] Y. Sandoz, C. Swinarski and B. Zimmermans (eds.), *o.c.* (note 221), p. 900.
[291] *Ibid.*, p. 901.
[292] *Ibid.*
[293] I. Cohn and G.S. Goodwin-Gill, *o.c.* (note 242), p. 94.
[294] CRC Committee, *General guidelines for periodic reports* (UN Doc. CRC/C/58, 1996), para. 124.
[295] CRC Committee, *General guidelines for periodic reports* (UN Doc. CRC/C/58, 1996), para. 127.

party to prevent the participation of children').[296] Rarely any insight is provided as to the way in which the feasibility of measures is evaluated.[297]

76. The absolute minimum of what a 'feasible measure to ensure that children do not take a direct part in hostilities' would be the prohibition to
'use' them. This will be discussed in Subsection 4.1, but it is already interesting to note here that the language of the ICC Statute points to this minimum or 'core obligation'. The relation between 'taking all feasible measures
to ensure non-participation', as laid down in Article 38§2 of the CRC, and
'using children to participate', as laid down in the ICC Statute, would be the
statement that any deliberate use of children is a violation of the duty to
take measures to prevent them from participating.[298] So protection under
the ICC Statute is in this perspective—the criminalized character set aside—
even lower than the one provided for in Article 38§2 of the CRC.

77. Finally, it should be emphasized again that the duty 'to ensure' *inter alia*
means that States Parties remain to be fully responsible for the acts of non-
State actors such as rebellious groups and private companies. This has been
confirmed in several of the CRC Committee's concluding observations.[299]

4. Third Paragraph Part 1: Protection from Recruitment for Under-15s

78. This paragraph is by scholars often dealt with together with the previ-
ous one.[300] In fact, in the beginning both paragraphs were discussed by the
CRC drafters as one provision,[301] that was only at a later stage split up in
two. Given the structure of Article 38 of the CRC,[302] it could be argued that
it would have been better to keep one paragraph encompassing both: the
first part would have been the general reaffirmation of the applicability of
IHL, followed by a part on the use of children in hostilities and a part on

---

[296] CRC Committee, *Concluding Observations: Democratic Republic of the Congo* (UN Doc.
CRC/C/15/Add.153, 2001), para. 65.
[297] CRC Committee, *Concluding Observations: Paraguay* (UN Doc. CRC/C/15/Add.166, 2001),
para. 46: 'States Parties should punish armed forces involved in forcible recruitment'.
[298] A. Cassese, P. Gaeta and J.R.W.D. Jones (eds.), *The Rome Statute of the International Criminal
Court: a Commentary* Vol. I (Oxford, Oxford University Press, 2002), p. 416.
[299] *Cf. supra* No. 53. *E.g.* CRC Committee, *Concluding Observations: Burundi* (UN Doc.
CRC/C/15/Add.133, 2000), paras. 71–72; *Democratic Republic of the Congo* (UN Doc.
CRC/C/15/Add.153, 2001), para. 64.
[300] *Cf.* S. Detrick, *o.c.* (note 6), pp. 652–656; G. Van Bueren, *o.c.* (note 158), pp. 334–340.
[301] S. Detrick, *o.c.* (note 6), p. 652.
[302] *Cf. supra* No. 38.

the protection of civilian children. Nevertheless, there are some substantial differences which could justify the split-up. First of all, §2 creates the obligation for every State Party to make sure that no child is used in hostilities, not only as a member of its own armed forces but neither as a member of any other armed group involved in the conflict such as guerrilla and paramilitary groups,[303] no matter how big the *de facto* control of these groups may be[304]—whereas §3 only creates obligations for the States Parties themselves. In this sense, §2 requires more of States Parties than §3. On the other hand, §2 is only applicable in the event of an armed conflict ('hostilities')—whereas §3 also includes obligations to be fulfilled in peacetime: recruitment is prohibited, even in the absence of hostilities.[305] So in that sense, §3 sets a higher standard than §2.

4.1. Object: *Recruitment*

79. Among scholars, this simple word is the source of a lot of confusion as to its exact meaning. Trying to untie this confusion, some difficulties arise: for instance, the term 'recruitment' is usually combined with a whole series of adjectives, which makes it hard to distinguish to what extent—if any—the content of the adjective could already by implied by the noun.

80. 'Recruitment' as a single word is not only used in Article 38§3 of the CRC but also in the two Additional Protocols[306] and the African Children's Charter.[307] 'Recruitment' as part of a combination is used in the Child Soldiers Protocol ('compulsory recruitment'[308] and 'voluntary recruitment'),[309] ILO Convention 182[310] ('forced recruitment' and 'compulsory recruitment'), the Turku Declaration ('recruitment in and allowed to join the armed forces'). The ICC Statute mentions two different yet clearly related terms ('conscription' and 'enlistment').[311] Finally, the CRC Committee tends to use all

---

[303] *E.g.* CRC Committee, *Concluding Observations: Colombia* (UN Doc. CRC/C/15/Add.137, 2000), para. 54: the CRC Committee 'expresses deep concern at the very high numbers of children who have been forcibly recruited into guerrilla and paramilitary groups'.

[304] *E.g.* CRC Committee, *Concluding Observations: Sudan* (UN Doc. CRC/C/15/Add.190, 2002), para. 6. *Cf. supra* No. 54.

[305] *E.g.* CRC Committee, *Concluding Observations: Sweden* (UN Doc. CRC/C/15/Add.2, 1993), paras. 8 and 11.

[306] Article 77 para. 2 of the AP1 and Article 4 para. 3 (c) of the AP2.

[307] Article 22 para. 2 of the African Children's Charter.

[308] Article 2 of the Child Soldiers Protocol.

[309] Article 3 of the Child Soldiers Protocol.

[310] Article 3(a) of the ILO Convention 182.

[311] Articles 8 para. 2(b)(xxvi) and 8 para. 2(e)(vii) of the ICC Statute.

foregoing terms, in addition to many other related terms ('recruitment',[312] 'forcible recruitment',[313] 'conscription',[314] 'voluntary enlistment',[315] 'voluntary recruitment',[316] 'join the armed forces',[317] 'voluntary or forced recruitment',[318] 'military service',[319] 'drafting into'[320]) and all possible combinations of all these.[321]

81. When taking a closer look at this mass of words, soon will be revealed that each of these words or word combinations expresses a different means by which persons become members of armed forces or armed groups.[322] This can happen *compulsorily*, regulated in national legislation. This is also called 'conscription'. Secondly, this can happen *voluntarily*, whereby people spontaneously go and 'join the army', which is also referred to as 'enlistment'. Thus it could be argued that the frequently occurring phrase 'voluntary enlistment' is a pleonasm, adding up to confusion, albeit ironically enough probably used for clarifying purposes. The ICC Statute handily avoids interpretation problems by using these clear and uncontested words 'conscription' and 'enlistment'. Thirdly, becoming a member of the armed forces can happen *forcibly*: people are forced to join the armed forces by use of force outside the law, for instance in the form of abduction.[323]

82. Now the place of 'recruitment' within this scheme can be sought. The drafting history of the CRC shows that there have been suggestions of cer-

---

[312] *E.g.* CRC Committee, *Concluding Observations: Spain* (UN Doc. CRC/C/15/Add.28, 1994), para. 3.

[313] *E.g.* CRC Committee, *Concluding Observations: Colombia* (UN Doc. CRC/C/15/Add.137, 2000), para. 54.

[314] *E.g.* CRC Committee, *Concluding Observations: Benin* (UN Doc. CRC/C/15/Add.99, 1999), para. 14.

[315] *E.g.* CRC Committee, *Concluding Observations: Iraq* (UN Doc. CRC/C/15/Add.94, 1998), para. 15.

[316] *E.g.* CRC Committee, *Concluding Observations: Sierra Leone* (UN Doc. CRC/C/15/Add.116, 2000), para. 26.

[317] *E.g.* CRC Committee, *Concluding Observations: Guinea-Bissau* (UN Doc. CRC/C/15/Add.177, 2002), para. 19(b).

[318] *E.g.* CRC Committee, *Concluding Observations: Mozambique* (UN Doc. CRC/C/15/Add.172, 2002), para. 74.

[319] *E.g.* CRC Committee, *Concluding Observations: El Salvador* (UN Doc. CRC/C/15/Add.9, 1993), para. 10.

[320] *E.g.* CRC Committee, *Concluding Observations: Greece* (UN Doc. CRC/C/15/Add.170, 2002), para. 29(b).

[321] *E.g.* CRC Committee, *Concluding Observations: Sierra Leone* (UN Doc. CRC/C/15/Add.116, 2000), para. 26 (voluntary recruitment) and para. 27 (recruitment).

[322] Coalition to Stop the Use of Child Soldiers, *1379 Report*, available at <http://www.child-soldiers.org>.

[323] *Ibid.*

tain delegations to replace 'recruitment' by 'compulsory recruitment' or 'conscription',[324] and to differentiate between 'voluntary recruitment' by military schools and 'obligatory recruitment'[325]—as was later done in he Child Soldiers Protocol. As these ideas were not followed without any discussion, the conclusion could be drawn that 'recruitment' in the sense of Article 38§3 of the CRC is supposed to encompass both compulsory and voluntary recruitment, or both conscription and enlistment. In this way, 'recruitment' appears to be a generic term, covering different ways in which the recruitment can happen, as depicted above.

83. However, this is not an uncontested hypothesis. On the one hand, the UNICEF Handbook excludes conscription from the ambit of 'recruitment': according to this source, 'Article 38 permits the recruitment of under-18s, but conscription is not mentioned and should not form part of State law or practice'. It goes on to state that '[c]ompelling children to join armed forces amounts to a breach of article 35 (abduction) and article 32 (forced labour)'.[326] Concretely this seems to mean that, according to UNICEF, 'recruitment' by definition exclusively happens 'voluntarily', because 'the compelled joining of the armed forces' is 'abduction' or 'child labour' and not 'recruitment'. On the other hand, and completely contrary to the opinion of UNICEF, it could be maintained that 'recruitment' excludes 'the voluntary joining of the armed forces' and thus by definition happens 'compulsorily': the drafting history of Article 77§2 of AP1 reveals that, although the ICRC had originally proposed to explicitly mention 'voluntary enrolment',[327] this phrase was deliberately deleted in the final version. Géraldine Van Bueren derives from this omission that 'recruitment' necessarily implies its exclusively compulsory character, especially since the Fourth Geneva Convention[328] expressly uses the term 'voluntary enlistment' which implies a difference between recruitment and voluntary enlistment.[329] This explains the formulation used in the Turku Declaration,[330] in which is stated that children 'shall not be recruited in nor allowed to join the armed forces'.[331]

---

[324] S. Detrick (ed.), *o.c.* (note 162), p. 505.
[325] *Ibid.*, p. 510.
[326] R. Hodgkin and P. Newel, Implementation Handbook for the Convention on the Rights of the Child (New York, UNICEF, 2002), p. 572.
[327] Y. Sandoz, C. Swinarski and B. Zimmermans (eds.), *o.c.* (note 221), p. 900.
[328] Article 51 of the GC4.
[329] G. Van Bueren, *o.c.* (note 158), p. 337.
[330] *Cf. supra* No. 30.
[331] Article 10 of the Turku Declaration.

84. Still, a close analysis of the *Commentaries to the Additional Protocols* undoubtedly points to the clear wish of the authors to include voluntary enrolment within the scope of 'recruitment'.[332] More importantly, the text of these *Commentaries* is unambiguous relating to the similar provision in AP2: 'The principle of non-recruitment *also prohibits accepting voluntary enlistment*'.[333] Confirmation of this theory can be found in the language of ILO Convention 182 (mentioning 'forced or compulsory recruitment'[334] which implies that there is also such thing as 'voluntary recruitment') and of the CRC's own Child Soldiers Protocol, which explicitly differentiates between 'compulsory recruitment' and 'voluntary recruitment'. Here, too, 'recruitment' is the generic term encompassing compulsory and voluntary dimensions.[335]

85. Several children's rights activists agree with this approach, but add that recruitment can not only happen compulsorily or voluntarily, but also forcibly (or in a coerced or abusive way).[336] The CRC Committee seems to belong to this corner: it makes all sorts of recommendations regarding forcible or voluntary recruitment when assessing State Party compliance with Article 38§3 of the CRC. It can be concluded, therefore, that 'recruitment' in the sense of Article 38§3 of the CRC covers any way in which someone becomes a member of the armed forces: the compulsory way by conscription, the voluntary way by enlistment, and the forcible way by abduction.

86. Géraldine Van Bueren explicitly states that recruitment is not equal to abduction.[337] This is fully reconcilable with the above-mentioned definition of recruitment for 'abduction' is of course a term which is much broader than 'forcible recruitment'. Abduction can—unfortunately enough—happen in plenty of situations and not only in the context of armed forces or groups forcing children to join them. In the latter case, both Article 38§3 and Article 35 of the CRC apply. As proposed by UNICEF, also Article 32 of the CRC on child labour comes into play: the type of work typically done as a member of the armed forces can easily fit into the category of 'work that is likely to be hazardous or to interfere with the child's education, or to be harmful to the child's health or physical, mental, spiritual, moral or social development'. This is painfully illustrated by Ilene Cohn and Guy S. Goodwin-Gill

---

[332] Y. Sandoz, C. Swinarski and B. Zimmermans (eds.), *o.c.* (note 221), p. 901.
[333] *Ibid.*, p. 1379—emphasis added.
[334] Article 3(a) of the ILO Convention 182.
[335] *Cf.* also M.T. Dutli, 'Captured child combatants', *l.c.* (note 286), p. 421.
[336] I. Cohn and G.S. Goodwin-Gill, *o.c.* (note 242), p. 28.
[337] G. Van Bueren, *o.c.* (note 158), p. 337.

in their groundbreaking study on child soldiers, pointing to the impact of participation at the psychosocial level (trauma), at the physical level (injury) and at the educational level (lost school time and worsened employment opportunities).[338] In this light, ILO Convention 182 is an expression of the conviction of Member States that both compulsory and forcible recruitment qualify as a prohibited form of child labour. Yet at the same time, this approach causes a 'grey zone'. It can be dangerous to use the criterion of 'against the will of the child' to determine whether the child labour is prohibited or not, as the ILO does by excluding 'voluntary recruitment': the distinction between 'compulsory' and 'voluntary' recruitment is often hard to make.[339] Indirect coercive measures such as social pressure and the perspective of physical protection and access to food and shelter are commonly used by recruiters, which makes the dividing line between 'voluntary' and 'forced' recruitment sometimes very imprecise and ambiguous.[340] Bearing this in mind, it is all the more laudable that Article 38§3 of the CRC seems to apply to *all* types of recruitment, thereby avoiding having to assess the 'voluntary' character of becoming a member of the armed forces, while it is all the more regrettable that the Child Soldiers Protocol reintroduces a differentiated treatment of compulsory recruitment on the one hand and voluntary recruitment on the other hand.[341]

4.2. Right Holder: *Persons who Have Not Attained the Age of Fifteen Years*

87. The same fierce discussions as had taken place for the setting of the legal minimum age for the participation in hostilities, happened for the legal minimum age for the recruitment, albeit to a lesser extent,[342] leading to the same result: persons who are considered to be children under Article 1 of the CRC, can still be legitimately recruited into the armed forces of a State, as from the age of 15 years. This standard is similar to the one set in Article 77§2 of AP1 and Article 4§3(c) of AP2, and coincides with the language of the ICC Statute. It is also the starting point from which to raise the legal minimum age for 'voluntary recruitment' by armed forces under

---

[338] I. Cohn and G.S. Goodwin-Gill, *o.c.* (note 242), pp. 98–115.

[339] *Ibid.*, p. 23.

[340] A. Honwana, 'Innocent and Guilty: Child-Soldiers as Interstitial and Tactical Agents', reprinted in F. De Boeck, *Anthropology of Children and Youth* (Leuven, Acco, 2002), p. 73.

[341] In spite of the 'safeguard' mentioned in Article 3 para. 3(a) that the recruitment has to be 'genuinely voluntary', the distinction remains hard to make.

[342] S. Detrick (ed.), *o.c.* (note 162), pp. 502–517.

Article 3 of the Child Soldiers Protocol. The other relevant legal instruments maintain a higher standard: the African Children's Charter protects all people under the age of 18 years, while ILO Convention 182 also prohibits the forced or compulsory recruitment of under-18s.

88. In line with this recent tendency to set the legal minimum age for recruitment at 18 years, as most recently established in the Child Soldiers Protocol, of which the CRC Committee has been an influential advocate, the CRC Committee's practice follows the straight-18 approach, for all types of recruitment: 'The Committee is concerned at the low age of 15 for voluntary enlistment in the armed forces.[343] [. . .] [It] recommends that the State party consider raising this to 18'.[344] It also takes this stance with regard to States Parties that allow children to be recruited with parental consent,[345] recommending them to set a minimum age of 18 years, 'without any possibility of recruitment below that age, even with parental consent'.[346] These are clear examples of the progressive functioning of the CRC Committee, as it actually disapproves of a standard literally provided for in the CRC itself, a standard resulted from the above-mentioned fierce discussions among drafting delegates.

4.3. State Party Obligations: *To Refrain from*

89. Since this obligation only concerns the State Party itself, as opposed to the obligation laid down in Article 38§2 of the CRC,[347] it is logical that it is put in an absolute way. This is clearly a negative duty, a duty *not to do*, which makes it immediately executable.[348] The CRC Committee is formal in this respect, and moreover expects the 'straight-18' approach from all States Parties.[349]

90. In the event that children under 15 years are recruited anyway, which goes against Article 38§3, the CRC Committee recommends to end this

---

[343] CRC Committee, *Concluding Observations: Bhutan* (UN Doc. CRC/C/15/Add.157, 2001), para. 54.

[344] CRC Committee, *Concluding Observations: Bhutan* (UN Doc. CRC/C/15/Add.157, 2001), para. 55.

[345] CRC Committee, *Concluding Observations: Sierra Leone* (UN Doc. CRC/C/15/Add.116, 2000), para. 26; *Cameroon* (UN Doc. CRC/C/15/Add.164, 2001), paras. 23–24(c).

[346] CRC Committee, *Concluding Observations: Cameroon* (UN Doc. CRC/C/15/Add.164, 2001), para. 24(c).

[347] *Cf. supra* Section 3.

[348] M. Bossuyt, 'La distinction juridique entre les droits civils et politiques et les droits économiques, sociaux et culturels', *Revue des droits de l'homme*, 1975, pp. 790–791.

[349] *Cf. supra* No. 67 and Subsection 3.2.

recruitment[350] and furthermore emphasizes the importance of demobilization and reintegration of child soldiers, in accordance with Article 39 of the CRC.[351]

5. Third Paragraph Part 2: Protection from Recruitment for Under-18s

5.1. Object: *The Priority Rule*

91. According to the *Commentaries to the Additional Protocols*, the obligation to recruit among the oldest first ('the priority rule'),[352] is the result of a compromise between those in favour of 15 years as an age limit and those in favour of 18 years.[353] By way of gesture towards the latter, the priority rule was added to Article 77§2 of AP1. About a decade later, the drafters of Article 38§3 of the CRC faced the same scenario. Of a Swedish proposal which—with a view to ensuring the consistency with existing IHL—contained amendments concerning the replacement of 'feasible measures' by 'necessary measures', the establishment of the minimum legal age for participation in hostilities at 18 years instead of 15 years, the prohibition of every type of participation instead of only of direct participation, and the insertion of the priority rule, only the last one was adopted.[354] As if the Working Group tried to make up for all the lost opportunities.

92. Nevertheless it is better to have the rule than not to have it as is the case in both high- and low-intensity non-international armed conflicts: not only common Article 3 of the Geneva Conventions but also Article 4§3(e) of AP2 lack a provision similar to the priority rule. As mentioned, Article 77§2 of AP1 does oblige States that are recruiting among persons between 15 and 18 years old, to endeavour to give priority to those who are oldest. Both the *ratio legis* and the formulation used are exactly the same in Article

---

[350] *E.g.* CRC Committee, *Concluding Observations: Sudan* (UN Doc. CRC/C/15/Add.190, 2002), para. 60 (a).

[351] *E.g.* CRC Committee, *Concluding Observations: Guatemala* (UN Doc. CRC/C/15/Add.58, 1996), para. 39; *Mexico* (UN Doc. CRC/C/15/Add.112, 1999), para. 20; *Burundi* (UN Doc. CRC/C/15/Add.133, 2000), para. 72; *Cambodia* (UN Doc. CRC/C/15/Add.128, 2000), paras. 58–59; *Sudan* (UN Doc. CRC/C/15/Add.190, 2002), paras. 59–60.

[352] This notion is of course not to be confused with the rule that in times of distress, children should receive relief first, which could also be called a 'priority rule', *cf.* Article III of the 1924 Declaration of the Rights of the Child, and Principle 8 of the 1959 Declaration of the Rights of the Child.

[353] Y. Sandoz, C. Swinarski and B. Zimmermans (eds.), *o.c.* (note 221), p. 901.

[354] S. Detrick (ed.), *o.c.* (note 162), p. 509.

77§2 of AP1 and Article 38§3 of the CRC. The only difference is, again, that the first necessarily requires the existence of an armed conflict—as AP1 is only applicable in armed conflicts, which is reflected by the phrase 'Parties to the conflict' used in its Article 77§2—whereas Article 38§3 of the CRC, as stated above, also creates obligations for States Parties in peacetime. Furthermore, this article extends the applicability of the priority rule to non-international armed conflicts. In this respect, Article 38§3 of the CRC is actually an advancement of established IHL norms. Still it must be said that a violation of the priority rule is not punishable under the ICC Statute (both in non-international and international armed conflicts) and also not a grave breach within the meaning of Articles 85 and 86 of AP1 (in international armed conflicts).

93. The priority rule is sometimes invoked by the CRC Committee, although it, as already often mentioned, consistently calls upon States Parties to adopt the 'straight-18' approach.[355] In its concluding observations on the United Kingdom, for instance, the CRC Committee recommends that the United Kingdom '[w]hile it recruits persons who have attained the age of 16 years but who have not attained the age of 18 years, endeavour to give priority to those who are oldest in light of article 38, paragraph 3, of the Convention'.[356] This is a clear application of the priority rule, albeit starting from the age of 16 and not 15 as stated in Article 38§3 of the CRC—another example of the CRC Committee fulfilling its role as the ultimate children's rights advocate endlessly striving for the highest standard. Here, too, the CRC Committee calls upon the United Kingdom to follow a 'straight-18' policy, stating that '[it recommends that the United Kingdom] strengthen and increase its efforts to recruit persons of 18 years and above'.[357]

94. So it is clear that at least from the CRC Committee's point of view, the priority rule should be thought of as a temporary measure, awaiting for the world to finally take the 'straight-18' approach. ILO Convention 182 and especially the African Children's Charter are already in that position, therefore not needing the priority rule. The Child Soldiers Protocol, on the contrary, only puts forward the legal minimum age of 18 years for compulsory recruitment, which means that there should be some sort of protection for

---

[355] *E.g.* CRC Committee, *Concluding Observations: Netherlands* (UN Doc. CRC/C/15/Add.114, 1999), para. 24.
[356] CRC Committee, *Concluding Observations: United Kingdom* (UN Doc. CRC/C/15/Add.288, 2002), para. 53(b).
[357] *Ibid.*

those who are not 18 yet but have 'chosen' to join the armed forces—not armed groups, as those should never recruit persons who are not 18 yet.[358] This 'special protection', as it is called in Article 3§3 of this Protocol, consists of four 'safeguards': it must be ensured that the recruitment is genuinely voluntary and carried out with the informed consent of the person's parents or legal guardians, and that the persons are fully informed of the duties involved in such military service and provide reliable proof of age prior to acceptance into national military service. As can be noticed, the priority rule is not part of the safeguards to be ensured. In any case, Article 3§3 of the Child Soldiers Protocol may be difficult to implement in practice for the reasons outlined above.[359]

5.2. Right Holder: *Persons who Have Attained the Age of Fifteen Years but who Have Not Attained the Age of Eighteen Years*

95. The Child Soldiers Protocol does have the advantage of raising the minimum legal age for compulsory recruitment to 18 years.[360] The minimum legal age for voluntary recruitment is raised as well, but to a lesser extent than the former: according to its Article 2§1, States Parties have to raise this age as a minimum to sixteen years.[361] Being better than nothing, it is regrettable that the drafters could not agree on fixing the 'straight-18' approach in a legally binding international instrument. Furthermore, as just noted, the Child Soldiers Protocol does not require States Parties to endeavour to give priority to those who are oldest, which in this respect lowers the standard set in Article 38§3 of the CRC—especially in light of the possibility for States to ratify this Protocol without being a party to the CRC.[362]

96. Once more the practical problems concerning birth registration must be recalled here.[363] As discussed in Subsection 5.1, the CRC Committee does

---

[358] Article 4 of the Child Soldiers Protocol.

[359] *Cf. supra* No. 86 on the boundary between compulsory and voluntary recruitment. *Cf.* also D. Helle, 'Optional Protocol on the involvement of children in armed conflict to the Convention on the Rights of the Child', *l.c.* (note 248), p. 805.

[360] Articles 1 and 4 of the Child Soldiers Protocol.

[361] D. Helle, 'Optional Protocol on the involvement of children in armed conflict to the Convention on the Rights of the Child', *l.c.* (note 248), p. 805.

[362] Article 9 para. 1 of the Child Soldiers Protocol reads as follows: 'The present Protocol is open for signature by any State that is a party to the Convention [on the Rights of the Child] *or has signed it*' (emphasis added).

[363] D. Helle, 'Optional Protocol on the involvement of children in armed conflict to the Convention on the Rights of the Child', *l.c.* (note 248), p. 805.

not refer to the priority rule without pointing to the highly preferred 'straight-18' approach, making sure the highest standard is applied.[364]

5.3. State Party Obligations: *To Endeavour*

97. Not any resistance has been voiced during the drafting process of Article 38§3 of the CRC to the term 'endeavour', not even from critical actors like the ICRC or the Swedish delegation.[365] This is probably due to pragmatism, as there were enough more pressing issues to be raised in the Working Groups, and, at a different level, given the inevitable practical problems one is faced when trying to enforce such a rule, for instance with regard to birth registration. Still, some opposition to this particular wording would have been understandable, thinking of the above-mentioned fact that this sentence is the result of a compromise between a minimum legal age of 15 years and one of 18 years—where it is obvious that the weakest standard has prevailed. It could be argued that the already meagre 'safeguard' accorded to 15- to 18-year-olds deserved a much stronger obligation for States Parties.

98. At first sight, the obligation to 'endeavour' looks like the weakest one within the whole of Article 38 of the CRC. After all, this 'obligation' is an obligation purely regarding conduct not regarding result, as has been pointed out in the *Commentaries to the Additional Protocols:*[366] States Parties have to 'try', to 'make an effort' to apply the priority rule. This is thus a merely subjective and barely controllable notion. Nevertheless, IHL seems to attach a meaning to this obligation which to a certain extent gives some substance to this otherwise rather insignificant obligation.

99. The *Commentaries to the Additional Protocols* clarify the scope of the obligation to 'endeavour', as used in common Article 3 of the Geneva Conventions: 'The provision does not merely offer a convenient possibility, but makes an *urgent request*, points to a duty'.[367] Concretely, this means, for instance, that the obligation laid down in Article 6§1 of AP1 to 'endeavour to train qualified personnel to facilitate the application of the [Geneva] Conventions and of [the First Additional Protocol]', covers the duty for all States Parties to 'establish a system of self-control capable of guaranteeing respect for the

---

[364] CRC Committee, *Concluding Observations: United Kingdom* (UN Doc. CRC/C/15/Add.288, 2002), para. 53(b).
[365] S. Detrick (ed.), *o.c.* (note 162), pp. 502–517.
[366] Y. Sandoz, C. Swinarski and B. Zimmermans (eds.), *o.c.* (note 221), p. 95.
[367] J. Pictet, *o.c.* (note 126), p. 42, emphasis added.

obligations entered upon, under the best possible conditions'.[368] By way of analogy this could imply that States Parties are obliged under Article 38§3 of the CRC to establish a system guaranteeing respect for the obligation to apply the priority rule, such as the training of recruiting personnel to systematically check upon the age of recruits.

6. Fourth Paragraph: Protection of Civilians

6.1. Object: *Protection and Care*

100. As explained in Section 2, dealing with the first paragraph of Article 38 of the CRC, child civilians (up to a certain age) do not only benefit from being protected from participation in hostilities and recruitment, as laid down in the second and third paragraph of this article. They are also the subjects of other measures of protection, to be outlined below. In the first place, they receive the same protection as all civilians (general protection), and secondly, IHL also contains some provisions specifically addressing child-related issues.

101. The general protection measures for the civilian child cover a wide range of provisions: in international armed conflicts they are protected persons under Article 4 of the Fourth Geneva Convention, which states the basic principle of humane treatment, including respect of life and physical and moral integrity, and forbidding, *inter alia*, coercion, corporal punishments, torture, collective penalties, and reprisals.[369] In accordance with AP1, civilian children also benefit from the rules on the conduct of hostilities that lay down, *inter alia*, the principle of distinction and the prohibition of attacks directed against the civilian population.[370] In low-intensity non-international armed conflicts, civilian children fall under common Article 3 of the Geneva Conventions, which provides persons not taking active part in the hostilities with some fundamental guarantees. Those include the right to humane treatment, and the right to life and to dignity. Where AP2 is applicable,[371] the fundamental principles on the conduct hostilities as mentioned above must be respected.[372]

---

[368] Y. Sandoz, C. Swinarski and B. Zimmermans (eds.), *o.c.* (note 221), p. 95.
[369] Articles 27–34 of the GC4; Article 75 of the AP1.
[370] Articles 48 and 51 of the AP1.
[371] *Cf. supra* No. 28.
[372] Article 4 of the AP2.

102. Above the general protection, children also receive special protection by simple virtue of being a child.[373] Next to some special protection measures against the effects of hostilities,[374] most provisions deal with the protection of the individual: the right to care and aid,[375] the issue of family unity,[376] special care for orphaned or separated children,[377] the preservation of the cultural environment of the child,[378] education,[379] personal rights such as the child's nationality,[380] special treatment for children deprived of their liberty,[381] and the absolute prohibition of the infliction of the death penalty.[382]

103. When taking a look at the substance, and sometimes even the form, of the enumerated protection measures, it is clear that a considerable part of these measures to a certain extent overlaps human rights. As explained, in times of armed conflict human rights remain in principle applicable—including economic, social and cultural rights as was pointed out by the CRC Committee. Notwithstanding the dual nature of State Party implementation obligations stated in Article 4 of the CRC, whereby economic, social and cultural rights are granted a significantly lower status than civil and political rights, the CRC Committee maintains that States Parties must take adequate measures to ensure the full implementation of the former category of rights.[383]

104. It is not a surprise to note that the CRC Committee categorizes the lack of, for instance, education as a consequence of an armed conflict as a violation of Article 28 of the CRC,[384] where it would have been perfectly possible to claim that this is a violation of Article 38§4 of the CRC, since IHL also states that 'children shall receive education', both in international[385]

---

[373] J. de Preux, 'Special protection of women and children', *International Review of the Red Cross* 248, 1985, p. 292.

[374] Articles 8(a), 17 and 78 of the AP1; Article 4 para. 3 (e) of the AP2.

[375] Articles 23, 70, 81, 85, 89 and 91 of the GC4; Articles 8 and 77 of the AP1; Article 4 para. 3 of the AP2.

[376] Articles 24–25, 75, 82 and 136–140 of the GC4; Article 4 para. 3 (b) of the AP2.

[377] Article 26 of the GC4.

[378] Articles 24 and 50 of the GC4; Article 78 para. 2 of the AP1; Article 4 para. 3 (a) of the AP2.

[379] Article 94 of the GC4; Article 4 para. 3 (a) of the AP2.

[380] Article 50 of the GC4.

[381] Articles 76 and 119 of the GC4.

[382] Article 68 of the GC4; Article 77 para. 5 of the AP1; Article 6 of the AP2.

[383] *E.g.* CRC Committee, *Concluding Observations: Azerbaijan* (UN Doc. CRC/C/15/Add.77, 1997), para. 12.

[384] *E.g.* CRC Committee, *Concluding Observations: Azerbaijan* (UN Doc. CRC/C/15/Add.77, 1997), para. 25.

[385] Articles 50 and 94 of the GC4.

and non-international[386] armed conflicts. This is also true for the occurrence of torture in the context of an armed conflict:[387] the CRC Committee seems to prefer to label this as a violation of Article 37 of the CRC and not as a violation of Article 38 of the CRC linked with the fundamental guarantee children have under IHL to be treated humanely and not subjected to torture.[388] Another example is family reunification: in spite of the clear rule existing under IHL for parties to a conflict to facilitate the reuniting of families dispersed as a result of an armed conflict,[389] the issue of internally displaced, unaccompanied and abandoned children is seen in terms of Article 10[390] or Article 22 of the CRC.[391]

105. Positive is the fact that this is a confirmation of the above-mentioned theory that the rights as laid down in the CRC are in principle non-derogable. Contrary to what is the case with other human rights instruments, the CRC cannot be derogated from in times of public emergency.[392] But on the other hand, sometimes the standards set in IHL are higher than those from the CRC, while the CRC Committee does not automatically invoke IHL in those cases. This could be seen as a lost opportunity: through the application of Article 38 of the CRC—especially its first and fourth paragraph—the CRC Committee could test States Parties' report by IHL norms which in some situations are the most conducive for the realisation of the rights of the child. This is the case with, for instance, the protection of children by the rules on the conduct of hostilities. Although international human rights law is silent on this issue,[393] the CRC Committee mentions the relevant IHL rules only very rarely.[394]

---

[386] Article 4 para. 3(a) of the AP2.

[387] E.g. CRC Committee, *Concluding Observations: Sierra Leone* (UN Doc. CRC/C/15/Add.116, 2000), paras. 44–45.

[388] Articles 75(b) and 77 para. 1 of the AP1; Articles 4 para. 2(e) and 4 para. 3 of the AP2.

[389] Article 74 of the AP1.

[390] E.g. CRC Committee, *Concluding Observations: Ethiopia* (UN Doc. CRC/C/15/Add.144, 2001), paras. 42–43.

[391] E.g. CRC Committee, *Concluding Observations: Democratic Republic of the Congo* (UN Doc. CRC/C/15/Add.153, 2001), paras. 62–63.

[392] Cf. supra No. 12.

[393] Of course this could be seen as a violation of the right to life—but it is clear that IHL is much more detailed and demanding as to the obligations of the parties to the conflict (i.e. not only States, as opposed to human rights obligations).

[394] One example found: CRC Committee, *Concluding Observations: Sudan* (UN Doc. CRC/C/15/Add.190, 2002), para. 59(c): 'While noting the demobilization of some children, the Committee is deeply concerned that [...] Government forces have conducted *indiscriminate bombing of civilian areas, including of food stocks*'—emphasis added. One notices that the CRC Committee does not even refer to the relevant article (Article 51 of the AP1).

106. The only systematic exception to the prevalence of human rights in the CRC Committee's practice seems to be the high priority given to the compliance of States Parties to the Ottawa Convention on landmines.[395] The Ottawa Convention is a recent instrument related to methods and means of combat, which is a 'pure' IHL matter. The CRC Committee does not only refer to de-mining efforts, prevention and rehabilitation for victims of mine-related accidents, it even expresses its opinion on States Parties advocating the Ottawa Convention[396] or being reluctant to ratify it[397]—something which it normally only does for UN instruments such as ILO Convention 138[398] and 182, or the Optional Protocols to the CRC. Although the Ottawa Convention is indeed a 'unique' instrument in terms of media attention and links to human rights (such as the right to life but also the rights of disabled children), this could be seen as a sign of a more IHL-oriented approach taken by the CRC Committee.

6.2. Right Holder: *Civilian Children Affected by an Armed Conflict*

107. The age limit to be used to understand who is a 'child' has been discussed previously in Subsection 2.2. The same reasoning can be applied for the fourth paragraph, defining 'child' in accordance with Article 1 of the CRC.

108. In the famous 'Machel Report',[399] it is described in what ways children are affected by armed conflict: children are abandoned[400] or displaced,[401] become orphan,[402] do not have full access to health care or education, . . .[403]

---

[395] *E.g.* CRC Committee, *Concluding Observations: Kuwait* (UN Doc. CRC/C/15/Add.96, 1998), para. 30; *Nicaragua* (UN Doc. CRC/C/15/Add.108, 1999), para. 38; *Georgia* (UN Doc. CRC/C/15/Add.124, 2000), paras. 58–59; *Uzbekistan* (UN Doc. CRC/C/15/Add.167, 2001), para. 61; *Guinea-Bissau* (UN Doc. CRC/C/15/Add.177, 2002), paras. 48–49.

[396] *E.g.* CRC Committee, *Concluding Observations: Germany* (UN Doc. CRC/C/15/Add.43, 1995), para. 4; *Mozambique* (UN Doc. CRC/C/15/Add.172, 2002), para. 4; *Germany* (UN Doc. CRC/C/15/226, 2004), para. 62.

[397] *E.g.* CRC Committee, *Concluding Observations: Kuwait* (UN Doc. CRC/C/15/Add.96, 1998), para. 30; *Georgia* (UN Doc. CRC/C/15/Add.59, 2000); *Israel* (UN Doc. CRC/C/15/Add.195, 2002), para. 59(d).

[398] ILO Convention concerning Minimum Age for Admission to Employment (C138 Minimum Age Convention), entered into force 19 June 1976.

[399] *Cf. supra* No. 1.

[400] *E.g.* CRC Committee, *Concluding Observations: El Salvador* (UN Doc. CRC/C/15/Add.9, 1993), para. 11; *Kuwait* (UN Doc. CRC/C/15/Add.96, 1998), para. 8.

[401] *E.g.* CRC Committee, *Concluding Observations: El Salvador* (UN Doc. CRC/C/15/Add.9, 1993), para. 11.

[402] *E.g.* CRC Committee, *Concluding Observations: Algeria* (UN Doc. CRC/C/15/Add.76, 1997), para. 27.

[403] *E.g.* CRC Committee, *Concluding Observations: Yugoslavia* (UN Doc. CRC/C/15/Add.49, 1996), para. 5.

This report has clearly inspired the CRC Committee to take this perspective when discussing children and armed conflict, stressing the 'extremely negative'[404] and 'traumatic'[405] impact of armed conflict on children, and pointing to the disastrous effect the latter has on the human rights of children,[406] even after it has ended as long as 12 years ago.[407]

109. However, not all children affected by armed conflict fall within the scope of Article 38§4 of the CRC. This paragraph obliges States Parties only to take measures to ensure protection and care *in accordance with their obligations under IHL to protect the civilian population*. Therefore, only child civilians are the right holders of this paragraph. It must be reiterated how unfortunate it is that Article 38 of the CRC does not explicitly protect the rights of child combatants as well.[408]

6.3. State Party Obligations: *To Take All Feasible Measures to Ensure (in accordance with their obligations under IHL to protect the civilian population)*

110. There is a general consensus on Article 38§4 of the CRC: everybody agrees it is a lowering of the standards set in the Geneva Conventions and their Additional Protocols.[409] The use of the phrase 'feasible measures' was already controversial in the context of the participation in hostilities[410]— yet this was nothing compared to the agitation caused when the discussion moved to the protection of the civilian population. During the drafting of this paragraph, the ICRC had made strong statements on the fact that *all* provisions in the Geneva Conventions and their Additional Protocols were formulated in stronger language than the proposed 'feasible measures' that States Parties were supposed to take.[411]

---

[404] *E.g.* CRC Committee, *Concluding Observations: Colombia* (UN Doc. CRC/C/15/Add.137, 2000), para. 55.

[405] *E.g.* CRC Committee, *Concluding Observations: Sri Lanka* (UN Doc. CRC/C/15/Add.40, 1995), para. 44.

[406] *E.g* CRC Committee, *Concluding Observations: Colombia* (UN Doc. CRC/C/15/Add.137, 2000), para. 9; *Sudan* (UN Doc. CRC/C/15/Add.190, 2002), para. 6.

[407] CRC Committee, *Concluding Observations: El Salvador* (UN Doc. CRC/C/15/Add.232, 2004), para. 4.

[408] *Cf. supra* No. 42.

[409] J. Kuper, *International Law Concerning Child Civilians in Armed Conflict* (Oxford, Clarendon Press, 1997), p. 104; S. Detrick (ed.), *o.c.* (note 162), pp. 514–516; G. Van Bueren, *o.c.* (note 158), p. 342.

[410] *Cf. supra* Subsection 3.3.

[411] J. Kuper, *o.c.* (note 411), p. 104.

111. The *travaux préparatoires* as described by Sharon Detrick reveal a rather shocking decision procedure used:[412] after lengthy discussions as to the proper adjective to describe State Party obligations, the Chairman 'noted that there was opposition to the Working Group to the adoption of the word "necessary" and observed that the Working Group could not agree on a compromise word as an alternative to "necessary" or "feasible". Taking into account the fact that no participants in the Working Group had expressed opposition to the adoption of the word "feasible" and the fact that some delegations had indicated that they were willing to support a consensus in favour of the word, the Chairman suggested that it might be solution for the Working Group to adopt that word. No participants in the Working Group objected to the solution put forward by the Chairman'.[413] Interesting detail topping off this story is the request done by the Swedish representative to exceptionally receive a transcript of the meeting 'since we adopted an article [. . .] on the basis of a debate which I do not think is reflected in that decision'.[414]

112. Even when taking into account the potentially somewhat broader interpretation one could give to the scope of the obligation to take 'feasible measures' as described above in Subsection 3.3, it must be acknowledged that it is indeed a very weak obligation compared to the relevant sister articles in the Fourth Geneva Convention,[415] which all contain unambiguous language such as 'shall', 'may not', or 'shall take the necessary steps'. Quite understandably, the outcome of this drafting discussion was one of the seeds for the campaign to adopt the Child Soldiers Protocol.[416]

113. The CRC Committee has not missed out on any opportunity to show which position it takes in this debate. In its concluding observations it consistently uses a formulation that is much stronger than the provisions of Article 38§4 of the CRC: 'The Committee urges [Ethiopia] *to make every effort to ensure that [. . .]* children are protected from the effects of armed conflict',[417] or 'The Committee reiterates its recommendation [. . .] that [Peru] *continue taking effective measures* to protect children against the negative impact of internal violence, including the establishment of rehabilitation measures for

---

[412] S. Detrick (ed.), *o.c.* (162), pp 514–516.
[413] S. Detrick (ed.), *o.c.* (note 162), p. 516.
[414] Cited in J. Kuper, *o.c.* (note 411), p. 105.
[415] *Inter alia* Articles 20 para. 1, 23 para. 1, 50 para. 2 and 68 para. 4 of the GC4.
[416] J. Kuper, *o.c.* (note 411), p. 106.
[417] CRC Committee, *Concluding Observations: Ethiopia* (UN Doc. CRC/C/15/Add.144, 2001), para. 69—emphasis added.

child victims of this violence',[418] or 'In light of articles 38 and 39 of the Convention, the Committee recommends that [Georgia] *take all appropriate measures to ensure* the protection and care of children affected by armed conflict'.[419] These are clearly all expressions demanding more from States Parties than the strict letter of the CRC—which is maybe the spirit of the CRC.

114. One particular sentence has become standardized in the CRC Committee's concluding observations: 'The Committee recommends that the State Party *at all times ensure respect for human rights and humanitarian law aimed at the protection and care of children in armed conflict*',[420] which constitutes a much more considerable obligation for States Parties. First of all, the word 'children' seems to include child combatants, who are still entitled to protection and care.[421] Furthermore, the phrase 'at all times' suggests a non-derogable, absolute obligation, while this together with 'human rights and humanitarian law' reconfirms the duty of States Parties to respect both bodies of law in a parallel manner. 'Ensure respect', finally, triggers the multitude of obligations mentioned above in the part on Article 38§1 of the CRC, such as the responsibility for non-State actors and for other States and all the obligations to be fulfilled in peacetime.

7. Conclusion

115. This contribution examined the meaning of the terms used in Article 38 of the CRC. Another question relates to the meaning of Article 38 as a whole: does this provision fill a gap in the protection of the rights of children in armed conflicts? Having outlined its scope, it seems that the potential added value of Article 38 is to be found in its hybrid character, being an IHL provision in a human rights treaty.

Having an IHL provision in the CRC makes it possible to extend certain IHL features to human rights law. For instance, it opens the possibility of rendering a human rights provision applicable to non-State actors. As the accountability of non-State actors such as transnational corporations with

---

[418] CRC Committee, *Concluding Observations: Peru* (UN Doc. CRC/C/15/Add.120, 2000), para. 18—emphasis added.

[419] CRC Committee, *Concluding Observations: Georgia* (UN Doc. CRC/C/15/Add.214, 2000), para. 59—emphasis added.

[420] *E.g.* CRC Committee, *Concluding Observations: Armenia* (UN Doc. CRC/C/15/Add.119, 2000), para. 49; *India* (UN Doc. CRC/C/15/Add.115, 2000), para. 64; CRC *Bhutan* (UN Doc. CRC/C/15/Add.157, 2001), para. 57(a); *Uzbekistan* (UN Doc. CRC/C/15/Add.167, 2001), para. 62(a).

[421] *Cf. supra* No. 43.

regard to human rights[422] is still under scrutiny, this constitutes a major advancement in the use of the CRC. This is particularly significant given the fact that the majority of armed conflicts nowadays are non-international. Moreover, the typical IHL duty to 'ensure respect' implies the extra guarantees for the protection of the rights of children in armed conflicts described above. Thus, States are obliged to take measures to make sure that other States respect IHL, not only by granting financial resources, but also by condemning violations where needed.[423]

Being part of a human rights treaty, Article 38 of the CRC can also influence the interpretation of IHL. The clear definition of the child, used throughout the CRC including its Article 38§1, questions the distinction made in IHL between combatants and civilians. The view that also child combatants are entitled to the protection of their rights is supported by the CRC Committee.

And it is this human rights monitoring mechanism that probably contributes most to the significance of Article 38: even though the CRC Committee's concluding observations and general comments are not legally binding, they are granted a considerable moral and political value. They can actually change States Parties policies and legislation. Especially bearing in mind the generally progressive stance taken by the CRC Committee, for instance by consistently advocating the 'straight-18' approach, this Committee could make a difference. By asking States Parties both for implementation measures in law and disaggregated data qualifying practice on the ground,[424] the CRC Committee has a great potential to fill the most important gap still left in the protection of the rights of children in armed conflicts. For in fact, the normative framework of those children is, with all its deficiencies and weaknesses, relatively good and complete.[425] The practice on the battlefield, however, can still be most horrid. The gap that needs to be addressed most urgently, is therefore that between law and practice.[426] It is hoped that the CRC Committee continues to be a vital actor in filling this gap that affects millions of children in the world.

---

[422] Cf. e.g. the Norms on the responsibilities of transnational corporations and other business enterprises with regard to human rights (UN Doc. E/CN.4/Sub.2/2003/12/Rev.2, 2003), approved by the Sub-Commission on the Promotion and Protection of Human Rights, Resolution 2003/16 (UN Doc. E/CN.4/Sub.2/2003/43, 2003).

[423] According to some, even the use of force might be justified: S. Bula-Bula, 'Le parapluie humanitaire de l'enfant', Revue Interdisciplinaire des droits de l'homme I, No. 1, 1995, p. 15.

[424] CRC Committee, General guidelines for periodic reports (UN Doc. CRC/C/58, 1996), para. 7.

[425] T.A. van Baarda, 'De rechtspositie van kinderen in gewapende conflicten: Een algemene inleiding', in: E. Verhellen (ed.), Rechten van kinderen in de wereld: Verzamelde lezingen naar aanleiding van de postacademische vorming 'Rechten van het kind' Universiteit Gent, academiejaar 1994-1995 (Gent, Centrum voor de rechten van het kind, 1996), p. 86.

[426] T. Meron, 'The Humanization of Humanitarian Law', l.c. (note 56), p. 276.